Helping Elderly Victims

Columbia Studies of Social Gerontology and Aging

Columbia Studies of Social Gerontology and Aging
Abraham Monk, General Editor

Rosalie S. Wolf and Karl A. Pillemer

Helping Elderly Victims

THE REALITY OF ELDER ABUSE

COLUMBIA UNIVERSITY PRESS   NEW YORK

32.55

61699

HV
6626.3
W65
1989

Columbia University Press
New York   Guildford, Surrey
Copyright © 1989 Columbia University Press
All rights reserved

Library of Congress Cataloging-in-Publication Data
Wolf, Rosalie S.
Helping elderly victims: the reality of elder abuse
Rosalie S. Wolf and Karl A. Pillemer.
p. cm.—(Columbia studies of social gerontology and aging)
Bibliography: p.
Includes index.
ISBN (invalid) 0-231-06484-5.   ISBN (invalid) 0-231-06484-3 (pbk.)
1. Aged—United States—Abuse of.   2. Abused aged—United States.
3. Abused aged—Services for—United States.
4. Social work with the aged—United States.
I. Pillemer, Karl A.   II. Title.   III. Series.
HV6626.3.W65 1989   88-28255
362.6—dc19   CIP

Printed in the United States of America

Casebound editions of Columbia University Press books are Smyth-sewn
and printed on permanent and durable acid-free paper

In memory of my husband, Wallace—R. S. W.

To my wife, Clare, and my children, Hannah and Sarah—K. A. P.

Contents

Contents

Preface

W HEN we were first approached by the Massachusetts Executive Office of Elder Affairs in 1980 to design the evaluation component for a proposal on elder abuse, little did we realize how extensive the assignment would become and how it would influence our careers. By the end of the three-year project period, we had completed a dozen different tasks. In this volume we have chosen to focus on three of the major components of the evaluation: an analysis of data on 328 cases of abuse and neglect; an organizational assessment of the model projects' structure, operation and outcome; and a case-control study involving 42 victims of physical abuse. To set the stage for the presentation and analysis of the data that follow, we present below a brief description of the Model Projects and how they came into existence.

The three projects were initiated in 1981 with funds from the Administration on Aging. Although there was very little information on elder abuse at that time on which to base a demonstration project, the interest of Congress and the concern of the Commissioner on Aging prompted the Administration on Aging to allocate a portion of its 1980 discretionary budget to support several experimental model projects on elder abuse. The objectives of the demonstrations were: 1) to determine the extent of elderly abuse in a geographic area; 2) to develop knowledge of existing responses; 3) to demonstrate improved mechanisms for reporting and investigating treatment and prevention programs; and 4) to design social and legal remedies to restore the rights and well-being of abused elderly. Each of the three projects selected for funding approached these tasks in a different way.

The Massachusetts Executive Office of Elder Affairs (EOEA) had been engaged in both the study and treatment of the problem for several years. In 1978, it financed a state survey of professionals and paraprofessionals on the maltreatment of the elderly. Conducted by Legal Research and Services for the Elderly of Boston (O'Malley et al. 1979), the survey documented the existence of elder abuse in the state. EOEA also supported a community-based agency, Elder Home Care Services of the Worcester Area (EHC) that had established a crisis intervention program for serving abused and neglected elders. According to the Massachusetts proposal, a special elder abuse unit would be created within EHC that would extend the agency's case management capability to include interagency agreements for 24-hour response, temporary shelter, family counseling, and other needed services. The objective of the Massachusetts project was to plan and coordinate an elder abuse and neglect program that offered health, mental health, social and legal services, and housing to abused and neglected elders, as well as to abusers.

The Metropolitan Commission on Aging (MCOA) of Onondaga County, New York, proposed to design and implement a service system that utilized the existing county human service infrastructure. For administrative and management purposes, the project would be subcontracted to Alliance, a local affiliate of Catholic Charities of Syracuse that had experience in the delivery of services to abused children and their families. The objective as specified in the commission's proposal was to work with the community's social and legal systems toward the development of a comprehensive and coordinated network for the treatment and prevention of elderly abuse.

As both a statewide Area Agency on Aging and a state unit on aging, the Rhode Island Department of Elderly Affairs (DEA) had a unique opportunity to demonstrate a statewide comprehensive response system for elderly abuse. In its application, the department proposed to develop a data base documenting the prevalence of elder abuse, to increase public awareness, to coordinate a state mandated reporting system, and to offer counseling and assistance to the abused and abuser.

Shortly after the announcement of the awards, at the suggestion of the Region I Office of the Administration on Aging, a joint meeting of the staff of the three projects was held to discuss the evaluation procedures. Although the proposals from the Metropolitan Commission and the Rhode

Island Department of Elderly Affairs contained references to the development of a data system and collection of information on prevalence and incidence of abuse, only the Massachusetts application included an evaluation plan. The interest of the staff of the other two projects in adopting this methodology led to the development of single evaluation design for the three Model Projects. A unified evaluation framework was created by incorporating all project objectives into a set of researchable questions and by using similar definitions, common reporting forms, and standardized procedures.

This book reports on the results of the evaluation, which, to our knowledge, represented the first attempt to systematically compare different intervention programs for elder abuse and neglect. Like all program evaluations, "real world" problems at times intruded into the carefully planned research design. Despite such imperfections, the Model Projects generated a wealth of information on characteristics of victims and abusers, on factors related to the occurrence of elder abuse and neglect, and on the relative success of different types of intervention programs.

SCOPE

We have divided this book into four parts. The first, entitled Introduction: Background and Theories, has two chapters. Chapter 1 begins with a description of the factors that have contributed to the growing concern about elder abuse and neglect and proceeds with a historical account of domestic violence, noting the similarities and differences in the "discovery" and conceptualization of child, spouse and elder abuse. It ends with a response to critics who question the utility or validity of treating elder abuse as a special social problem.

The first section of chapter 2 is devoted to the definitions of "abuse" and "neglect" that have varied widely in the research literature and in legislation. For the present study, a five-category definition was used, consisting of: physical, psychological, and material abuse and active and passive neglect. Chapter 2 also reviews early prevalence studies and presents the findings from a more recent random sample survey of elder abuse and neglect. It closes with a description of five risk factors for elder abuse and neglect drawn from the sociological, psychological, and gerontological literature on family relations. They are: 1) intra-individual dynamics; 2) intergenerational transmission of violent behavior; 3) dependency and exchange relations between abuser and abused; 4) external stress; and 5) social isolation.

Part 2 focuses on the victims, perpetrators, and the abuse situation itself. The method used for obtaining data on the 328 cases seen by the Model Projects introduces chapter 3. Descriptive findings are presented, including the characteristics of the victims and perpetrators, the types of abuse and neglect and their manifestations, and the situational characteristics. With the exception of "intergenerational transmission of violent behavior," for which there were insufficient data, support is found for all the risk factors. The picture of elder abuse and neglect that begins to emerge, however, favors intra-individual dynamics and dependency as the more plausible explanatory factors.

Two comparative analyses are described in chapter 4. The first is an examination of the relationship of each of the risk factors to the five types of maltreatment. The results produce five profiles, which on closer scrutiny represent three distinct types. One is associated with physical and psychological abuse in which the victim suffers from emotional problems but is relatively independent. In these cases, the perpetrator is apt to have a history of psychopathology and to be dependent on the victim, particularly for economic support. The second pattern is characteristic of neglect, and involves an older unmarried victim who is very dependent. The perpetrator neither has psychological problems nor is financially dependent on the victim but finds caring for the victim to be very stressful. The third profile is that of material abuse. The perpetrators have financial problems, sometimes traceable to a history of alcohol abuse. For them, the single, lonely elder is an easy target for exploitation. The relationship of risk factors to types of abuse is also explored in a second analysis, but, this time, the comparison is between spouse and parent abuse cases. Again, there are differences. The spouse perpetrators are more closely identified with physical-psychological abuse, and the adult children perpetrators with neglect or material exploitation.

The relationships described in chapter 4 are explored in greater detail in chapter 5, using a subsample of victims of physical abuse. The approach to the research differs from previous efforts because it focuses on one type of mistreatment, involves direct interviews with abused persons rather than relying on professional reports, and incorporates a matched comparison group of non-abused elders. Case material is presented to illustrate the scope and depth of the conflicts that exist between the victims and perpetrators.

The final chapter in part 2 examines the treatment strategies used by the project staff, changes in status of the victims over the course of the project, and factors that contribute to the resolution of the cases. All three projects recorded a large decrease in the number and severity of the manifestations of abuse and neglect and a significant reduction in the threat which they posed for the victim. For about one-quarter of the cases there was little or no success in resolving the abuse situation; for slightly less than one-half, the elimination of abuse resulted from separation of the victim and the perpetrator through nursing home placement, death, hospitalization or relocation into new community residences.

The introduction to part 3, Organizational Analysis, sets forth the methodology that is used in evaluating the Model Projects. Chapters 7, 8, and 9 describe the major components of the three projects in considerable detail, employing case examples and depicting typical client pathways. The historical factors that influenced the development of the projects and issues of interagency coordination provide the context for the assessment and intervention process.

Part 4 presents the final chapter of the book. It includes a summary of previously presented findings about the nature of elder abuse and neglect, the impact of the treatment strategies, and the feasibility of model replication, followed by a discussion of the implications of these findings with regard to abuse and neglect research, practice, and policy. Drawing on the results of the Model Project study, the book ends with a reiteration of the need to address elder abuse as a special social problem.

Acknowledgments

THIS book could never have been written without the generous assistance of many persons. From the first days of the evaluation to the time this manuscript was completed, a number of individuals gave us their enthusiastic support and cooperation. We are extremely grateful to them all.

Our major debt is to the staff of the three Model Projects: Edward J. McCarthy and Valerie Kennedy in Worcester, Massachusetts; Patricia Cridland and Meme Woolever in Syracuse, New York; and Joyce Hall and Patricia Hird in Providence, Rhode Island. Several state and local officials were involved in overseeing the projects, including Kent Boynton, Massachusetts Department of Elder Affairs; Lois Green, Elder Home Care Services of Worcester Area, Inc.; Roslyn Bilford, Metropolitan Commission on Aging of Onandaga County, New York; and Anna M. Tucker, Rhode Island Department of Elderly Affairs.

We also acknowledge the Administration on Aging, which funded the evaluation of the three Model Projects. Within the Administration on Aging, special thanks are due to Bill Neth, who providing unflagging and enthusiastic assistance throughout the grant period. The opinions and points of view expressed here are, of course, our own, and do not necessarily represent official Administration on Aging policy.

Several persons at the University of Massachusetts Medical Center provided invaluable assistance. In particular, Michael A. Godkin developed some of the key measures and data collection instruments for the study, and worked intensively on the data analyses, especially those described in the first half of chapter 4. Former Research Associate Cecille P. Strugnel also made important contributions in the initial phase of the evaluation. Computer programming was ably conducted by Marilyn Shapleigh and Molly Mainville. Steven Baker was most generous in providing statistical consultation. We also thank our secretaries, Ellen DeMetre, Doris Primmer, Paula Zecco, and Debbie Pinney. Caroline Youska, Student Intern, assisted greatly in the case-control study described in chapter 5. Special words of appreciation are due to Susan McMurray Anderson, Risa Breckman, Andrea Nevins, Pamela Ansell, and Nanci Burns, who read and commented on the manuscript.

Finally, we would like to express our gratitude to our institutions, which have provided encouragement for the preparation of this book. Rosalie Wolf acknowledges the University Center on Aging, University of Massachusetts Medical Center, Gari Lesnoff-Caravaglia, executive director. Karl Pillemer is grateful to the Family Research Laboratory at the University of New Hampshire for its support of research and writing on elder abuse. In particular, thanks are due to J. Jill Suitor, David Finkelhor, Gerald Hotaling, Murray Straus, Linda Williams, and Scott Feld for being such supportive colleagues.

Helping Elderly Victims

PART ONE

Introduction, Background, and Risk Factors

1

Introducing the Issues

T HE past two decades have seen the shattering of a number of myths regarding the American family. Contrary to the popular view of the family as a safe haven for its members, critics have portrayed it as oppressive to women (Thorne and Yalom 1982; Chodorow 1978), damaging to children (Straus, Gelles, and Steinmetz 1980), and unfulfilling for men (Lasch 1977). The general thrust of the criticism extends as far back as Freud, who identified the fierce battles that can lie beneath seemingly harmonious family life. Many contemporary scholars agree that there is a tremendous discrepancy between the ideal family that is portrayed in the media and that many Americans believe in, and the troubled reality that families often experience (Skolnick 1987).

The shattering of family myths has also occurred in gerontology. It was widely believed that in earlier times, a "Golden Age" of family life existed for the elderly, in which three or more generations lived together in happy extended families. As members of these family units, the aged were lovingly cared for, and reciprocally assisted the household to the best of their abilities. In his seminal book on the topic, historian Peter Laslett (1965) identified this view as the "world we have lost" syndrome, which involves the sense that a "before" period exists in which the elderly were revered and played valuable roles, and an "after" period, in which the aged became scorned and isolated.

Extensive data now exist demonstrating that this Golden Age is actually a myth (see Nydegger 1983). In fact, substantial family conflict with the aged existed in preindustrial times. Frequently, such conflict occurred over property, as sons waited eagerly for their fathers to die so they could inherit land. Historical evidence even points to serious intergenerational violence in past times, including parricide (Stearns 1986). In addition, legend and literature paint a picture of severe conflict with the aged, from ancient Greek creation myths, to Shakespeare, to Maupassant (Reinharz 1986).

A second myth has also come under attack: that there exist "Golden Isles" in which the elderly are universally revered and respected. In particular, it is widely believed that in preliterate or nonindustrial societies the aged occupy an enviable status. Mounting anthropological evidence, however, indicates that severe conflict with the aged, and serious maltreatment of them, exists in these cultures. Several anthropologists have documented that killing the aged or abandoning them to die is a more common practice than might be supposed (Foner 1985; Glascock and Feinman 1981). Even when treatment of the aged is not so severe, strains exist in nonindustrial societies between the frail elderly and younger people. As Foner sums up the evidence: "the frail old in nonindustrial societies . . . are not in an enviable position" (1985:398).

In sum, problems in the aging family seem to know no temporal or cultural boundaries. Only recently, however, have social gerontologists, psychologists, and others begun to focus specifically on family conflict and the elderly. One reason for this, perhaps, is that many scholars have devoted considerable energy to combating the myth that families today abandon their elderly relatives (see Shanas 1979; Brody 1985). Indeed, students of the aging family at present emphasize the importance of a continued positive role for kin in the lives of the elderly. Family, it is held, can give a sense of social and psychological continuity throughout life. Additionally, this view highlights the role of kin in providing personalized interaction for the elderly, which is crucial to their sense of identity. Emotional support and concrete goods and services are seen as coming most appropriately from family members.

In fact, there is no question that many families behave responsibly toward aged members. Over the past decade, however, a growing body of research has demonstrated that husband-wife and parent-child relations in later life can be severely strained. An especially compelling issue involves those situations in which the elderly suffer from direct maltreatment by family members, or in which their needs for care are left unmet. These problems have come to be termed "elder abuse" and "elder neglect."

The problem of elder abuse and neglect first came to the public's attention approximately ten years ago. The ensuing years have seen the development of intervention programs at the state and local levels, and the expression of major concern by the federal government (Salend et al. 1984). Reports on elder abuse have appeared in many mass media publications and on national television. To provide a proper context for the research findings that occupy much of the remainder of this book, it will be useful to review the evolution of current concern about elder abuse. Our discussion begins with a look at the "discovery" of child abuse and wife abuse and then turns to the recent attention paid to elder maltreatment.

HISTORICAL CONTEXT

Child abuse has gone on for much of recorded history, and attempts to combat it in this country stretch back into the 1800s (Radbill 1975). The present wave of interest in this problem, however, is the longest-lasting one so far. Beginning in 1946, radiologists began reporting the curious finding that subdural hematoma and abnormal x-rays of the long bones were associated with one another in some cases; that is, children sometimes reported with both conditions. Caffey (1946) related these conditions to early childhood trauma. It was left primarily to Kempe et al. (1962) to assert that this trauma was willfully inflicted by parents. In his classic study of the "battered child syndrome," Kempe called the medical community's attention to the startling problem of physical child abuse.

The mobilization of effort to combat child abuse in the subsequent decades was monumental. By 1968, all fifty states had implemented legislation mandating reporting of child abuse and providing protective services for children. In the 1970s, the federal Child Abuse Prevention and Treatment Act was enacted, and the National Center on Child Abuse and Neglect was created. The federal government has made millions of dollars available to child abuse programs, and states have spent similar amounts on protective services and public education.

It is important to note that child abuse was "discovered" by professionals, and attempts to solve this problem have originated and been managed primarily by the medical, legal, and social work professions. In fact, Newberger and Bourne (1978) stress this point, arguing that child abuse since the early 1960s has been extensively "legalized" and "medicalized." They even cite evidence that physicians adopted child abuse as a medical problem in order to increase prestige and expand their role. Child welfare agencies were also eager to intervene in this "new" problem (see also Nelson 1984).

Such has not been the case with battered women. The development of programs in the area of wife abuse has been tied instead to the feminist movement, and has in large part existed outside of the formal service network. Unlike abused children, who quickly found champions in the legal community, throughout the 1960s and 1970s battered women encountered what Myers has termed "a grim tale of judicial and police non-response" (1980:339). Sociologists also tended to ignore the problem of husband-wife violence, due to family sociology's general lack of attention to family violence, and to the casual public acceptance of wife abuse as something "normal" (Straus, Gelles, and Steinmetz 1980).

Works by such feminist authors as Dworkin (1974) and Dobash and Dobash (1981) helped to focus public attention on the problem, as have many other publications by activists in the women's movement. In addition, concrete services to battered women have been largely initiated by feminist groups. For example, Kalmuss and Straus (1983) found that the number of services available to abused women in a state was significantly related to the level of feminist organization in that state.

We thus have two very different examples of the discovery of a type of abuse and its consequent labeling as a social problem (Spector and Kitsuse 1977). In one case, medical, legal, and social work professionals were instrumental in calling attention to the abuse, while in the other, the problem only came to national attention after it became linked to a powerful grass-roots social movement.

Elder abuse appears to fit the child abuse discovery pattern most closely. Although a few activist groups have called attention to the problem, formal service agencies and professionals have been quick to monopolize this issue. Callahan (1981) raises the possibility that elder abuse programs have developed "because there is a supply of professionals looking for new markets—resources in search of needs." While their interest was probably not so consciously self-serving, health and human service workers have dominated as writers on the topic, witnesses at federal hearings, and advocates for state legislation (Salend et al. 1984).

As noted, elder abuse and neglect are phenomena which appear to have existed throughout history. Why then has such unprecedented professional and public attention been directed in the past few years to the issue of maltreatment of the elderly? While a precise answer to this question awaits further historical research, it is clear that at least the following four factors are important to some degree in this new attention.

First, there has been tremendous growth in the elderly population. The increase in the proportion of the elderly who are 75 years of age or older has been even more dramatic (Atchley 1987). This demographic shift has led to a concomitant increase in the number of people professionally and personally concerned about aging. In promoting social action on behalf of the elderly, advocates have drawn public attention to many areas where society's actual relationship to the aged belies its ideals. One such area is family life. Professionals who work with the elderly have pointed out that many problems of the elderly, including abuse and neglect by family members, can be expected to increase, simply because of the growth in the numbers of the aged.

A second factor related to the growth in the elderly population is the increasing political power of the aged. In recent decades, age-based organizations have grown in size and strength; some now number their members in the millions (Hudson and Binstock 1976; Atchley 1987). Politicians and other policy makers fear the exposure of elder abuse cases as they do incidents of child abuse: such events indicate a lack of concern for vulnerable individuals in society. The greater political attention paid to the aged is certainly an important impetus behind mandatory reporting laws and other state-level interventions.

Third, the resurgence of the women's movement in the 1970s has prompted an examination of myths about family life and an increasing recognition that the family can be extremely oppressive to some of its more vulnerable members. Since the middle of the last decade, the women's movement has conducted a major campaign of public awareness about wife abuse and family violence. Researchers allied with this movement have pointed out that, in spite of social preoccupations about crime by strangers, vulnerable family members are at greatest risk of victimization by intimates. These concerns have helped build a foundation for the interest in maltreatment of the elderly which followed.

A final source of interest in elder abuse is the increasing willingness of the state to intervene in family life. There has been enormous growth since the late 1960s in the portion of state bureaucracy dedicated to protecting vulnerable individuals. These "protective services" emerged primarily in reponse to concerns about disadvantaged, disabled, and maltreated children, and reflected new social standards about the quality of care children deserved. Protective service workers educated the public about these standards and legitimized a number of state interventions into family life, including: reporting laws which encouraged and required professionals (and even private citizens) to make official reports about suspected maltreated persons; investigatory procedures designed to substantiate reports of abuse; and state custody over vulnerable individuals to separate them from family and provide them with more secure environments. Already familiar with conducting these interventions on behalf of children, it was but a short step for state protective services to expand the domain of their advocacy to include the vulnerable elderly (Crystal 1986; Salend et al. 1984).

RECENT TRENDS IN ELDER ABUSE POLICY

The preceding discussion provides a general overview of the development of elder abuse as a social problem. However, in order to place the Model Projects study in proper perspective, it is also important to review specific activities of federal and state agencies on elder abuse. Overall, the record indicates a lack of federal leadership on this issue, which has led in turn to a host of individual state approaches to intervention.

The first public mention of elder abuse took place before a Congressional subcommittee in 1978. This testimony on the reported battering of parents served as the catalyst for a series of hearings the following year sponsored by the House Select Committee on Aging under the leadership of Representative Claude Pepper, and by the House and Senate Special Committees on Aging jointly in June 1980. As a result of those hearings and an intensive investigation by the House staff, a series of policy alternatives was proposed for action by the Congress, states and local communities (U.S. House of Representatives 1981).

The report recommended that the federal government assist the states in their efforts to deal with the problem by enacting the "Prevention, Identification, and Treatment of Elder Abuse Act." This act would have created a National Center on Elder Abuse under the Secretary of Health and Human Services for the purposes of compiling, publishing, and disseminating information about programs and special problems related to elder abuse, neglect, and exploitation. The center would have been authorized to conduct research into the causes, prevention, treatment, and national incidence of elder abuse, neglect and exploitation. In addition, the bill would have given assistance to states to provide for the reporting, investigation, assessment, and treatment of such events. This bill was not passed by Congress.

In 1985, a second influential document on elder abuse was released by the House Select Committee on Aging (1985). Spurred by a growing volume of mail documenting abuse of the elderly, the Subcommittee on Health and Long-Term Care initiated an inquiry to update what was known about the problem. Although there had been a significant increase in the number of states with legislation on elder abuse, the Subcommittee "was disturbed by the indications that elder abuse had not abated and perhaps was increasing" (p. 2). Furthermore, they found that only about 4.7 percent of the average state's total budget for protective services was allocated for the elderly (a reduction from the 1980 level) even though about 40 percent of all reported abuse cases involved adults and abused elders. The major source of federal funding for protective services, the Social Services Block Grant, had been reduced nearly one fifth by direct cuts and inflation in the intervening years.

The recommendation of the Select Committee was a restatement of the 1981 report: that the federal government should assist the states in their efforts to deal with the pervasive problem of elder abuse, using an approach analogous to that of the Child Abuse Prevention, Identification, and Treatment Act of 1974, which established a national center. The bill was refiled by Representative Oakar. Another piece of legislation, this time to establish a national task force to study the topic and determine means of prevention, identification, and treatment, was introduced by Senator Mark Andrews in the Senate and Representative Mario Biaggi in the House. However, the 99th Congress ended before any action could be taken on these measures.

Several other attempts at elder abuse legislation have taken place in Congress, but with at most only token success. It seems possible that the concern about elder abuse came too late to spur major congressional interest. As Nelson has noted in an insightful analysis of the development of child abuse legislation, by the early 1980s, Congress was no longer in the control of social liberals. A new budget process and hard economic times had altered the way in which issues were defined. Further, conservatives in the administration and in Congress shared the philosophy that problems such as child abuse and elder abuse were more appropriately addressed by the states. For these reasons, many in Congress balked at the reauthorization of the Child Abuse Prevention and Treatment Act in 1981, although it was eventually passed (Nelson 1984).

It was in this environment that elder abuse became an issue. No leadership emerged to shepherd bills through the Senate as then Senator Walter Mondale and others had done for child abuse legislation. In contrast to the child welfare advocates, proponents of elder abuse legislation were hampered by a lack of solid research on the topic. Most of the information in the House Select Committee on Aging reports was anecdotal. The few studies that formed the basis for the estimates of the incidence of the problem were flawed because of small, unrepresentative samples, inconsistent definitions, and poor methodology. Some concerns were also raised about the role of the state vis-à-vis the federal government and the authority of states to intervene in the lives of elders. Without adequate information concerning the extent, nature, and causes of the problem, it was difficult for legislators to determine which programs would be most appropriate.

In the absence of congressional leadership, federal agencies might have stepped in to fill the policy vacuum regarding elder abuse. However, neither the Administration on Aging, which is primarily concerned with social welfare issues, nor the National Institute on Aging, which is devoted to research, took on elder abuse as a major agenda item in the manner that the Children's Bureau had done with child abuse. To be sure, however, both agencies have funded elder abuse-related projects.

In 1978, the Administration on Aging supported two small exploratory research projects (Block and Sinnott 1979; Douglass, Hickey, and Noel 1980). Two years later, the agency funded two training conferences (Bergman 1981) and the three Model Projects already described (see Preface). More recently, the Administration on Aging provided grants for a number of elder abuse demonstration projects on information dissemination and public awareness and, in 1988, for a national aging resource center on elder abuse.

To date, only two projects on elder abuse have been financed by the National Institute on Aging. One grant was given to researchers at the University of New Hampshire to conduct a large-scale random sample survey of elder abuse in the greater Boston area (Pillemer and Finkelhor 1988). The other award went to Case Western Reserve University for a comparative study of child abuse and elder abuse cases (Korbin et al. 1987).

Although these activities appear to indicate a growing interest at the federal level, the reponse in proportion to public concern about the problem has been minimal at best. The Administration on Aging has neither the research oversight capability, the authority, nor the funds to carry out the type and extent of research activities on child abuse that were sponsored by the Children's Bureau two decades earlier. It has also been unable to coordinate a federal effort such as that of the National Center for Child Abuse and Neglect.

Without a national focus or a model statute, the states were left to develop their own laws. Some incorporated elder abuse into existing adult protective statutes or laws pertaining to elderly persons, while others passed special legislation. A few states created more than one law, and many have since amended the original versions. Salend et al. (1984), in their review of elder abuse legislation through 1980, reported that the major intent of the laws was to extend statutory authority to social service departments providing adult protection. Generally, social workers in public agencies provided the impetus for the legislation, although other groups were also involved. By 1988, all states had some form of legislation dealing with elder abuse.

A comparison of the definitions of maltreatment in the laws reveals wide differences. While most include "willful infliction of physical pain or injury" as a form of abuse, only about one in three include "unreasonable confinement"; and one in four, "illegal use of an adult" (including sexual abuse). Thirty of the statutes specify "willful infliction of mental anguish and psychological injury," and a few include "intimidation."

Neglect, mentioned in four out of five laws, is defined in various ways: as failure to "provide care and treatment," "to prevent physical or psychological pain or injury," "to protect and provide"; or as the "deprivation of essential services," which could mean food, clothing, and shelter as well as services that promote physical, intellectual, and emotional well-being. Self-neglect—the failure of the individual to provide for his or her own needs—was included in the laws of thirteen states. As Salend et al. (1984) note, the variety of definitions creates a situation in which state of residence is probably the most important factor in the designation of an abused elder. [1]

Because the laws reflect various social and political orientations, even criteria for "persons covered" are not the same. In twenty-eight states, the laws apply to "adults" who are impaired, incapacitated, or disabled; in thirteen states, persons "65 years and older"; six states, "60 years and older": and one state, "55 years and older." By 1987, all states had some form of legislation dealing with elder abuse.

The laws also vary in penalties for non-reporting. Thirty state laws contain penalties for failure to report, ranging from no fines up to fines of $1,000 and from no imprisonment to a maximum of six months. The others do not address the issue. Similarly, not all the laws include reference to the penalties for perpetrators: seventeen declare abuse or neglect a misdemeanor or a felony; four laws provide for restraining orders and/

1. Information concerning the state laws is derived from *A Comprehensive Analysis of State Policies and Practices Related to Elder Abuse*, prepared by the American Public Welfare Association and the National Association of State Units on Aging, 1986.

or injunctive relief. Many of the remaining laws provide for penalties through other statutes.

In summary, in spite of insufficient knowledge about the problem of elder abuse and ways to prevent and treat it, almost all state legislatures have been quick to get on the bandwagon. Nelson's analysis of the rapid adoption of state legislation for child abuse appears to hold true for elder abuse. She writes:

> In most cases, legislators acted from their hearts when they passed the first round of reporting laws. They considered the physical abuse of children disgusting, but few anticipated the relationship between reporting laws and the dramatic increase in demand for child protective services. . . . Legislators also viewed child abuse reporting laws as an opportunity for no-cost rectitude. They were able to condemn violence against children at no cost to the public purse—only one of the original laws carried an appropriation with it. (1984:76)

Although the record of funding elder abuse legislation was a little better than the initial response of the states to child abuse, essentially the politicians also found in elder abuse an issue with significant voter appeal that could be supported without additional appropriations.

From our review of the historical development of elder abuse policy, it is obvious that during the past decade there has been an acceleration of interest and activity in the issue, but most of it has occurred at the state level. Although over a dozen hearings relating to elder abuse were held by the U.S. House Select Committee on Aging during this period, they had little impact except as media events. Even the actions of the 100th Congress have been little more than symbolic: the passage of an amendment to Title III of the Older Americans Act requiring the states to establish elder abuse prevention programs, but providing no additional appropriation; and a resolution declaring the first week in May to be "National Older Americans Abuse Prevention Week." Nor have the various federal agencies that over the years expressed an interest in the problem been responsible for significant advancements in our understanding of the problem, its treatment, or prevention. Except for the two NIA studies, there has been no federally supported research since 1982.

Within this context, the experience of the Model Projects takes on greater importance, not only in adding to our knowledge about the nature of elder abuse, but also in suggesting directions for future policy and practice. The three Model Projects represent different ways in which two state units on aging and an area agency on aging responded to the problem. The results of the Model Projects study and its implications for research and policy are the subject of the remainder of this book. One final issue must still be addressed, however: Is elder abuse a "real" social problem, which deserves a special term, and a unique set of interventions?

ELDER ABUSE AS A SOCIAL PROBLEM

The social forces described above have combined to create considerable momentum behind efforts to identify and protect the maltreated elderly. Laws mandating the reporting of elder abuse have been passed in many jurisdictions. Special social agencies have been established to intervene in these cases. Many workers have been trained in techniques for identifying maltreated elders. In the midst of this activity, some critics have questioned whether the phenomenon of elderly people who are abused or neglected deserves a unique classification and a special term. One respected analyst has gone so far to state "Elder abuse is a dying non-issue whose time is past" (Callahan 1986:2).

Callahan, like other critics (Crystal 1986) argues that elder abuse is a problem that is difficult at best to define and that cannot be accurately measured. In addition, the objection is raised that the term "elder abuse" has been applied inappropriately to a host of family situations; to, as Callahan states, "situations that are often indistinguishable from the set of unhappy relationships that, unfortunately, affect many families" (Callahan 1986:2). He argues that we should move away from concern about elder abuse:

> The fact that violence and abuse exist and that older people are affected does not necessarily mean, however, that public policy is to be served by carving out that segment of abuse and developing specialized programs to deal with it. . . . In other words, does calling this behavior "elder abuse" help us move along in solving the problem . . . ? My answer to that question is that the well-being of the elderly will not be increased by a focus on elder abuse. (Callahan 1981:1)

As one of the authors has argued elsewhere (Finkelhor and Pillemer 1984), unlike Callahan, elder abuse does appear to us to constitute a distinct category of abuse, worthy of special attention. Such classification is justified by the special characteristics of the elderly, which affect their vulnerability to abuse and the nature of the abuse they suffer, and also by the nature of society's relationship to older persons. First, the aged as a group share characteristics that can create vulnerability to abuse. Many elderly persons (especially those over 75) experience increased frailty, especially as measured by their ability to carry out usual activities of daily living (bathing, dressing, walking, etc.). As Reichel notes, "The elderly generally show diminutions of physiologic capacities; in fact, the definition of aging is the decline in physiologic capacities or functions in an organism after the period of reproductive maturity" (1978:17). Many other gerontologists (see Hickey 1980; Ward 1984) have chronicled the heightened physical vulnerability of the elderly, as well as their greater likelihood of suffering from neurological impairments (Hendricks and Hendricks 1981). These physical vulnerabilities can exacerbate the risk of abuse as well as affect the nature and effects of abuse when it occurs.

Second, the elderly can be specially vulnerable to abuse because of their devalued social status. Butler (1975) observed that systematic sterotyping of and discrimination against old people exist (see also Levin and Levin 1980). This contributes to a loss of meaningful roles (Newell 1961) and to what Atchley (1987) has termed the "atrophy of opportunity," whereby society isolates older persons and no longer seeks their contributions. Mandatory retirement, which brings about the loss of occupational roles, further contributes to this process. This devaluation of elderly people can be seen as increasing their vulnerability to abuse as a class of individuals.

Third, the special categorization of elderly abuse also makes sense because of the relationship society has to the elderly. A service system exists that includes specialized professionals who relate to the elderly and deal with their needs and problems. Concern about abuse of the elderly has developed within this context, and it has legitimately evolved as a distinct problem, separate from other forms of family violence. Research and solutions will all develop within this distinct social matrix.

Finally, in spite of serious weaknesses in previous research (detailed in the following chapter) one thing has been learned from the many preliminary studies that have been conducted: elder abuse exists. Both studies of samples of clients from service agencies and general population surveys have uncovered elders who are severely maltreated by relatives, and who are unable to escape the situation. Callahan is correct that the problem has been overdefined, or, in his words, that there has been an attempt to "force the multiplicity of difficult human situations into an elder abuse framework" (1986:3). Because definitions have been overly broad, however, does not mean that a limited, precise definition of the problem cannot be created.

The process of investigation, assessment, and treatment of elder abuse cases requires training and knowledge not always available to workers in the field. To prepare individuals to work with these multiproblem families, we need to know a great deal more about the etiology of elder abuse and the legal and ethical implications of intervention. Moreover, we must learn what treatment and prevention strategies are the most effective. Contrary to the critics of the concept of elder abuse, it is our belief that older persons are especially vulnerable to certain kinds of maltreatment at the hands of family members, that this maltreatment can be defined and measured, and that the success of various interventions can be evaluated. It is the goal of the present volume to shed light on these issues.

2

Extent and Nature of Elder Abuse

D URING the past few years, there has been much speculation about
elder abuse, with some fairly extreme and unsupported statements being made about it and widely believed. States have re-
acted with a range of activites, sometimes in a rational and well-thought
out manner, and sometimes, unfortunately, in ways that have responded
more to political pressures than to the real needs of the elderly. In the
midst of this activity, considerable confusion exists regarding many of the
basic elements about elder abuse. How much elder abuse is there? Who
is most likely to be affected? What causes elder abuse? We are at an early
stage in uncovering answers to these questions.

In this chapter, we provide a general background for the later description of the characteristics of victims and abusers. We begin with definitional issues, and present the definitions used for the current study. Recent findings on the prevalence of elder abuse are then reviewed. Finally,
a theoretical discussion of risk factors is presented, which provides a
framework for our analysis of the correlates of elder abuse.

DEFINITIONS

Researchers have varied widely in the way in which they have defined
elder abuse. For example, Lau and Kosberg (1979) employ four categories

in their study: physical abuse, psychological abuse, material abuse, and violation of rights. Block and Sinnott (1979) include the first three categories, omit "violation of rights," and add "poor residential environment." The overlap is deceptive, however, because similarly named categories contain different types of injuries and abuse. Lau and Kosberg divide physical abuse into classes which may or may not involve injuries (direct beatings, lack of personal care, lack of food, lack of medical care, and lack of supervision), while Block and Sinnott use only types of injuries (bruises and welts, sprains and dislocations, malnutrition and freezing, abrasions, lacerations, cuts and punctures).

In another example, Hudson and Johnson (1987) note that Lau and Kosberg (1979) categorize "withholding of personal care" as physical abuse, while Douglass, Hickey, and Noel (1980) place it under "active neglect," and Sengstock and Liang (1982) subsume it under the category of "psychological neglect." As these examples indicate, definitional inconsistencies make it difficult to compare the outcomes of various studies.

The same is true of legislative definitions. Some states restrict their definitions to those instances in which there is an abuser; others include cases in which an old person is unable to meet his or her own needs ("self-neglect"). Some states specify that abuse victims must be mentally or physically impared or dependent, while others allow intervention with all types of elders.

It is at present impossible to resolve this definitional disarray, although several writers have made important attempts to clarify some specific points (Johnson 1986; O'Malley et al. 1986). In developing definitions for the Model Projects evaluation, we reviewed previous research efforts and state legislation, in order to identify those types of maltreatment on which their appeared to be greatest consensus. The definitions are presented in table 2.1.

First, all discussions of elder abuse include physical violence; there appears to be universal consensus that physical assault against an elder constitutes abusive behavior. Second, most of the research literature (although not all state laws) includes a category of "psychological," "emotional," or "mental" abuse. These terms are generally very vaguely defined, and the types of abusive behavior vary tremendously from study to study. Further, the category of psychological abuse has been criticized as including all types of family problems under the label "abuse" (Callahan 1982; Pedrick-Cornell and Gelles 1982; Crystal 1986). The persistent, widespread concern regarding this type of abuse, however, mandated that psychological abuse be included in the definition. We have restricted the concept to include intentionally abusive actions, to give the concept greater precision.

Third, material abuse was included as a category of maltreatment. This involved situations in which an elder's property or financial resources were stolen or misused. It is important to note, however, that the material abusers were necessarily a relative or acquaintance; robbery or theft by strangers was not included in the Model Project definitions.

Finally, the category of neglect appears in many studies and state laws, although it too is a controversial term. There appears to be general agreement that the intentional failure of a clearly designated caregiver to meet the needs of an elder constitutes neglect. A category has also been created, however, to cover situations in which older persons' care needs are not being met, due to the *absence* of a caregiver: so-called "self-neglect." This category has been criticized on the grounds that it does not represent a family maltreatment problem, but rather society's failure to meet the needs of the aged (Callahan 1982; Salend et al. 1984; Crystal 1986). The present study focused on domestic maltreatment by relatives or acquaintances. Therefore, the definition of neglect was limited to those sit-

---

TABLE 2.1: Definitions of abuse and neglect

Abuse:

Physical abuse: the infliction of physical pain or injury, or physical coercion, e.g., slapped, bruised, sexually molested, cut, burned, physically restrained, etc.

Psychological abuse: the infliction of mental anguish, e.g., called names, treated as a child, frightened, humiliated, intimidated, threatened, isolated, etc.

Material abuse: the illegal or improper exploitation and/or use of funds or other resources

Neglect:

Active neglect: refusal or failure to fulfill a caretaking obligation, INCLUDING a conscious and intentional attempt to inflict physical or emotional stress on the elder; e.g., deliberate abandonment or deliberate denial of food or health-related services

Passive neglect: refusal or failure to fulfill a caretaking obligation, EXCLUDING a conscious and intentional attempt to inflict physical or emotional distress on the elder; e.g., abandonment, non-provision of food, or health-related services because of inadequate knowledge, laziness, infirmity or disputing the value of prescribed services

---

uations that involved a caretaker's failure to assist an elderly person for whom they were responsible, either intentionally (active neglect) or unintentionally (passive neglect).

Thus, five major types of maltreatment were treated by the Model Projects: physical abuse, psychological abuse, material abuse, active neglect, and passive neglect. Other categories could have been included, and the abuse types defined differently. Because of the lack of consensus as to how elder abuse ought to be defined, it is only possible to construct clear definitions that involve mutually exclusive categories. As will be demonstrated in chapter 5, substantial differences were found between persons who fell into each of the various categories.

PREVALENCE OF ELDER ABUSE

Probably the most frequently asked question about elder abuse is: How much is there? It is important to obtain at least a preliminary idea of the extent of the problem, in order to effectively plan intervention strategies. Most of the research on elder abuse, however, has been conducted with cases that have been reported to agencies. It is widely recognized that these are highly selective samples, and that there is likely to be a large reservoir of unreported and undetected cases of elder abuse about which very little is known. Several attempts have been made to estimate the extent of elder abuse, based on surveys of the general population.

Block and Sinnott (1979) surveyed three groups by mail: community agencies, a random sample of elderly persons living in the community, and health and human service professionals. Respondents drawn from these sources were questioned about a range of types of maltreatment, including physical, financial, and emotional abuse, and neglect. The response rate was very low: only one agency in 24 responded, as did only 16 percent of the elderly and 31 percent of professionals. The elderly sample yielded a total of 26 reports of some form of abuse or neglect, or a rate of 40 abused elders per thousand.

Block and Sinnott's findings have been extrapolated to the total elderly population of the United States, resulting in a figure of over one million cases nationwide occurring each year. However, as Block and Sinnott note, this estimate may not be reliable. The response rate was so low (16 percent), and the final sample so small (73), as to invalidate the findings. Moreover, the survey appears to have asked about knowledge of abuse, rather than the actual experience. In spite of these methodological limitations, the 4 percent figure frequently appears in reports on elder abuse. Such reports often go on to describe this 4 percent figure as the "tip of the iceberg," and assert that a much higher percentage (up to 10 percent) of the elderly may be abused (see U.S. House SCA 1985).

In contrast, a very low estimate comes from a survey conducted by Gioglio and Blakemore (1983). They interviewed a random sample of 342 elderly persons in New Jersey. Only 5 of these respondents reported some form of maltreatment, which resulted in a rate of 15 victims per 1,000 elders. Problems exist in this survey, as well. With such a small sample, the confidence interval ranges from 2 cases per 1,000 at the lower limit to 28 cases per 1,000 at the upper limit. Further, only one of the five cases involved physical maltreatment; the other four cases of financial exploitation. Moreover, the New Jersey study did not use very precise measures of abuse, and relied on volunteer interviewers.

A more reliable survey was recently conducted (Pillemer and Finkelhor 1988), which attempted to assess the scope and nature of maltreatment of the elderly occurring in the community at large, including unreported and undetected elder abuse. The study was designed as a stratified random sample of all community-dwelling elderly persons (65 or older) in the Boston metropolitan area. In-person or telephone interviews were conducted with 2,020 elderly persons, with a response rate of 72 percent. Using a variety of measures, the survey inquired about respondents' personal experience of three types of maltreatment: physical violence, chronic verbal aggression, and neglect by family members and other persons close to them.

The survey found 63 elderly persons who had been maltreated in one or more of these three ways. This translated into a rate of 32 maltreated elderly per 1,000. Given the sample size, this yielded a 95 percent confidence interval of 25–39 maltreated elderly per thousand (that is, the true figure has a 95 percent chance of being in this range). With an elderly population in the Boston area of 345,827 in 1985, the authors estimated that there were between 8,646 and 13,487 abused and neglected elderly persons in that area. If a national survey were to find a similar rate, it would indicate between 701,000 and 1,093,560 abused elders in the nation as a whole. Rates were also calculated for each type of maltreatment: 20 per 1,000 for physical violence; 11 per 1,000 for verbal aggression, and 4 per 1,000 for neglect.

Rates of domestic abuse and neglect of the elderly may thus be somewhat lower than figures reported in the media and sometimes quoted by politicians. It also appears that rates of elder maltreatment are lower than other forms of family abuse. For example, a national survey of child abuse found that 110 children per thousand are seriously physically abused each year (Straus and Gelles 1986). It is encouraging to know that the majority of the elderly live free from serious domestic maltreatment.

Nevertheless, these somewhat lower prevalence figures do not indicate that elder abuse should be ignored as a social problem. Even prevalence rates that seem low by some standards can translate into impressive numbers of individuals in the population at large: potentially over a million abused elders in the United States as a whole. As the ensuing chapters will demonstrate, domestic abuse of the elderly can be a source of extreme suffering for those families in which it does occur. For this reason, widespread concern about the problem is not unwarranted.

It is clear, then that one area in which recent progress has been made is in estimating the prevalence of the problem. Such figures can do little, however, besides alerting us to the fact that the problem exists. In order to reduce the incidence of elder abuse, we must understand the factors that precipitate it. In particular, knowledge of risk factors must be improved before prevention programs that allow for early intervention with potentially abusive families can be developed. We now present a framework for understanding factors that may lead to elder abuse.

RISK FACTORS FOR ELDER ABUSE

We have seen that one goal of persons interested in elder abuse and neglect is a better understanding of the nature and extent of this type of maltreatment. There is difficulty, however, in employing existing research efforts to inform public policy, or even to establish a framework for future studies. It is worthwhile to summarize here some of the critical issues that need to be resolved by researchers. The first major problem in analyzing results from previous research on elder abuse and neglect has already been noted: poor definition of the term "elder abuse." Most of the studies are weakened by their undifferentiated treatment of various types of abuse and neglect. Second, different criteria have been used to determine the population at risk of "elder" abuse; some researchers have included persons under 60 years of age in their sample, while most others have limited their research to persons 60 (or 65) and over. Other investigators have restricted their studies to persons sharing a residence with the abusers (Block and Sinnott 1979), or to caretakers of the elderly

(Steinmetz and Amsden 1983), while O'Malley et al. (1979), Gioglio and Blakemore (1983), Wolf, Godkin, and Pillemer (1984), and others include all abused or neglected elders.

Third, the studies have employed widely differing methods, from Gioglio's (1983) random sample survey to Lau and Kosberg's (1979) review of patient records. This methodological inconsistency makes it particularly difficult to compare the findings of the studies. A fourth major drawback of many studies is their exclusive reliance on professional reports of cases of elder abuse and neglect.

Fifth, few of the studies described above included comparison groups in their designs. For this reason, the generalizations made by the researchers are necessarily suspect. For example, some investigators have asserted that the abused and neglected elderly tend to be physically and/ or mentally impaired. However, without a comparison group, it is impossible to know if they are more or less impaired than other persons.

Despite their methodological limitations, previous studies suggest some fairly consistent findings regarding the abused elderly. Most of the studies showed that abused individuals tended to be female, although in Pillemer and Finkelhor's (1988) research, victims were evenly divided between men and women. Abused elders have also generally been found to be disproportionately "old-old" (75 and over). Most studies have found that abused elders tend to suffer from a range of physical and mental impairments. Finally, it has been shown consistently that abused elders tend to live with the perpetrator of the abuse (see Pillemer and Finkelhor, 1988). These findings, sketchy as they are, are unfortunately the only ones that emerge reliably from the studies. Results relating to the frequency with which abuse occurs and the types of abuse most often found are virtually impossible to compare, due to the widely varying definitions employed. Further, few of the studies provide reliable evidence on risk factors for elder abuse.

In sum, a theoretical framework for understanding elder abuse cannot be derived from a previous research on elder abuse. There are two literatures, however, that may have the ability to predict the occurrence of abuse. First, findings from the study of child and spouse abuse may shed some light on elder abuse. In previous literature reviews, however, there has been a tendency to simply extend concepts relating to other forms of family violence to elder abuse. We believe it is necessary to include a second body of research as well; the more general literature on relations between spouses, and between elderly parents and adult children. Findings related to the determinants of the quality of family relationships of the elderly can provide important insights into elder abuse, especially in concert with family violence research. These two literatures are considered in the following pages.

Because the writings on these two topics are extensive, we have been quite selective in the review. Here, it is only possible to outline the most important issues in a general way (for a more complete discussion of risk factors, see Pillemer and Suitor 1988; Pillemer 1986). The areas which emerged from the review are as follows: 1) intra-individual dynamics; 2) intergenerational transmission of violent behavior; 3) dependency and exchange relations between abuser and abused; 4) external stress; 5) social isolation.

Intra-individual dynamics

This view emphasizes characteristics of the abuser, and in particular psychopathology, as primary causes of maltreatment. Interestingly, family researchers have found that psychological well-being is related to the general quality of family relationships. Thus, various measures of psychological well-being have been consistently associated with marital satisfaction both among the general population and specifically among the elderly. Andrews and Withey (1979) found respondents' evaluations of their marital relationships to be positively associated with measures of global well-being; Glenn and Weaver (1981) reported that marital happiness was strongly related to global happiness; and Lee (1978) showed that older persons' morale to be correlated with marital satisfaction. While the causal direction in these studies cannot be precisely determined, it seems persuasive that the psychological well-being of marriage partners affects the quality of relationships.

The existence of such a relationship has also been widely held in the literature on family violence. Many early investigations of child abuse held that abusive parents suffered from some kind of psychological disease. The cure for child abuse, in this view, was to treat the emotional illness (Gelles 1974). Some of these researchers—largely psychiatrists, social workers, and other clinicians—attributed abuse to "sadistic" personality traits (Young 1974), while others traced it to a flaw in the socialization process. Investigators of wife abuse also traced such behavior to psychopathological traits in the abuser (see Faulk 1974; Shainess 1975; Lion 1977).

A prominent critic of such intra-individual explanations is Gelles (1974), who argues that various writers are unable to agree as to which personality traits lead to abuse. He notes that many of these studies were not rigorous tests of the intra-individual hypothesis, but were instead after-the-fact explanations of deviant behavior that had already occurred. These problems are exacerbated by reliance on clinical samples, and failure to use' non-abuse comparison groups. Gelles goes on to call for an emphasis on social structural factors as important determinants of abuse, such as socioeconomic class, economic stress, and unemployment. In general, purely intra-individual explanations of abuse have been increasingly avoided by researchers (see Straus 1979b), although a recent comprehensive review of research on wife abuse again points toward intra-individual factors (Hotaling and Sugarman, 1986).

One intra-individual characteristic has been emphasized by some investigators: alcohol and drug abuse. A number of studies have now substantiated that a relationship between substance abuse and family violence exists (see Coleman and Straus 1981; Kantor and Straus 1986). Alcohol and drug consumption may diminish inhibitions against abusive acts, or may instead provide an excuse for violent behavior carried out intentionally. Case-control studies are necessary to demonstrate a causal role for substance abuse in domestic violence against the elderly.

It should also be noted that the dynamics of elder abuse may differ from other forms of family violence. In particular, elder abusers may be more likely to suffer from psychological problems. Some research has in fact provided evidence that persons who abuse the elderly are more likely to be developmentally disabled, mentally ill, or alcoholic (Lau and Kosberg 1979; Douglass, Hickey, and Noel 1980; Bristowe 1987; Anetzberger 1987; Finkelhor and Pillemer 1987).

Intergenerational transmission of violent behavior

It has by now become commonplace that victims of child abuse grow up to be abusers. In fact, many researchers have postulated that children learn to be violent in family settings, and use these learned behaviors when they become adults. This theory is sometimes summed up as a "cycle of violence." In one of the most extensive reviews of the spousal violence literature, Hotaling and Sugarman (1986) found that the cumulative research evidence does indeed identify witnessing parental violence during childhood as one of the strongest risk factors for wife abuse as an adult. In a national survey, Straus, Gelles, and Steinmetz (1980) found that the amount of physical punishment experienced as a child was positively associated with the rate of abusive violence to one's own children.

Based on the strength of such evidence, it is reasonable to postulate that elder abusers will also be more likely to have been raised in violent families. At present, however, no evidence exists to support this hypothesis. It is important to note that a significant difference exists between elder abuse on the one hand, and child abuse and spouse abuse on the other. Specifically, children who abuse elderly parents were not *themselves* abused as elderly parents; the "cycle of violence" must therefore take an alternative form. Rather than becoming an abuser because one was abused by someone else, the cycle becomes much more direct: the formerly abused child strikes out at his or her own abuser. This would appear to involve a different psychological process, one with elements of retaliation as well as imitation.

Dependency

Interestingly, two competing theories have arisen that relate dependency to elder abuse. The first emphasizes the role of caregiver stress as a risk factor for maltreatment; abuse is seen as resulting from the resentment generated by the increased dependency of an older person on a caretaker. The second theory stresses the reverse configuration: the continued dependency of the *abuser* on his or her victim. Each of these theories will be taken in turn.

Caregiver stress. The literature on the family relations of the elderly supports the notion that increased dependency of an old person leads to poor quality relationships with relatives. One of the most consistent findings is that parent's health is positively correlated with feelings of closeness and attachment between parents and their adult children (Baruch and Barnett 1983; Cicirelli 1981; Johnson and Bursk 1977). A likely reason for this is the effects of a decline in the parent's health on the prior flow of support between the generations. Adult children may have to increase their support to the parent, and possibly to accept the cessation of assistance from the parent.

In fact, studies have documented the negative effects of parental dependency. Cicirelli (1983a, 1983b) found negative feelings on the part of adult children when both parental dependency and the amount of help from the child were high. Similarly, a study by Adams (1968) revealed that affectional ties to widowed parents were weaker when adult children's help was not reciprocated. Thus, it appears that when adult children feel that the support relationship with a parent is inequitable, the quality of the relationship declines.

Many students of elder abuse have also emphasized the dependency of the victim on the abusive relative (see Steinmetz 1983; Steinmetz and Amsden 1983; Davidson 1979; Quinn and Tomita 1986). It is argued that families undergo stress when an elderly person becomes dependent upon his or her relatives for care. The burden of providing financial, physical, and emotional support produces severe stress on the caregiver. As the costs to the caregiver grow—and the rewards diminish—the exchange becomes perceived as unfair. According to this view, caregivers who do not have the ability to escape or ameliorate the situation may become abusive.

Abuser dependency. While the above theory appears plausible, there are few firm research findings to support it. It is clear from the gerontological literature that a substantial number of elderly persons are dependent on relatives (Cantor 1983; Brody 1985). However, as the prevalence findings mentioned earlier indicate, only a small minority of the elderly are abused. Therefore, no direct correlation can be assumed between the dependency of an elderly person and abuse.

Further, the investigations which have highlighted the dependency of the victims have generally had methodological weaknesses. In particular, they have not included control groups in their designs. It is well documented that the majority of the elderly suffer from one or more chronic conditions; it should therefore be of no surprise to learn that abused elders were somewhat impaired. Thus, it is not sufficient to note that abuse victims have some level of physical dependency. Instead, we must ask: are the abused elderly more ill or impaired than nonvictims? Do they depend on the abuser more than other elders depend on nonabusive relatives? In fact, a case-control study conducted by Phillips (1983) failed to find any difference in level of impairment between a group of elder abuse victims and a control group. More recently, Bristowe (1987) found abused elders to be less impaired than a control group.

Moreover, there is some evidence that a significant degree of dependency exists on the part of the abusers. The first such evidence came from Wolf, Strugnell, and Godkin (1982). These investigators surveyed community agencies in Massachusetts regarding elder abuse cases they had encountered. This study found a "web of mutual dependency" between abuser and abused. In two-thirds of the cases, the perpetrator was reported to be financially dependent on the victim. Hwalek, Sengstock, and Lawrence (1984), in a case-control study, also found that financial dependency of the abuser was an important risk factor in elder abuse. A study based on interviews with elder abusers also supports the hypothesis that the dependency of relatives, rather than the elder, is an important risk factor for abuse (Anetzberger 1987).

This finding that the continued dependency of an adult child or spouse upon an elderly relative is related to physical abuse may seem counter-intuitive. However, an explanation for these results can be derived from social exchange theory (Dowd 1975). A key concept in the social exchange perspective is that of *power*. Finkelhor, in his attempt to identify common features of family abuse, notes that abuse can occur as a response to perceived powerlessness. In fact, abusive acts "seem to be acts carried out by abusers to compensate for their perceived lack or loss of power" (1983:19). It may be that an adult child or other relative who is still dependent on an older person feels especially powerless, as this dependency strongly violates society's expectations for normal adult behavior. This perceived *lack* of power on the part of the abuser appears to have more explanatory power than the view that the abuser holds much power in the relationship, as a caretaker would (see Pillemer 1985b, for a more complete discussion).

As this discussion indicates, the role of dependency in elder abuse deserves serious consideration. In this section, we have posed the two views of dependency as competing hypotheses: that *either* dependence of abuser *or* abused may lead to elder maltreatment. Perhaps a better way to conceptualize the issue is to view a serious imbalance of dependency in either direction as a potential risk factor. In fact, research on middle-aged couples has found that marital satisfaction and adjustment decline when one or both partners perceive that the relationship is inequitable (Davidson, Balswick, and Halverson 1983; Yogev and Brett 1985). Similarly, Cohler (1983) asserts that continued feelings of family responsibility by older persons toward their children are associated with low morale and psychological distress.

Researchers must explore the role of both types of inequity in elder abuse. Does an elderly person come to make excessive demands on caregivers? Or are the abusers persons who have remained dependent on the victims into later life? In order to shed light on this issue, investigations of such factors as the need for assistance of the abused, subjective caregiver burden on the part of the abuser, and mutual dependence between the two must be carried out. Analyses presented in later chapters of this book provide data on some of these issues.

External stress

A number of investigators have found a positive relationship between external stress (as differentiated from the stress that results from interpersonal relationships in the family) and child and wife abuse (Gil 1971; Justice and Justice 1976; Straus, Gelles, and Steinmetz 1980). A stress perspective on abuse can be seen as an alternative to the theories previously discussed. In Gelles and Straus' (1979) terms, it is a "socio-cultural" theory—rather than a social-psychological or intra-individual one—in that it emphasizes social structural, macrolevel variables like unemployment or economic conditions. However, the social stress model alone cannot explain elder abuse, for it does not explain why some families respond to stress with abuse and others do not. To date, no systematic exploration has established a link between stress and elder abuse, although Sengstock and Liang (1982) and Finkelhor and Pillemer (1987) provide preliminary evidence that such a relationship exists. Based on the strength of findings relating stress to other forms of family violence, this area would also appear to be an important one for future investigators.

Social isolation

Social isolation has also been found to be characteristic of families in which other forms of domestic violence occur (Gelles 1972; Gil 1971; Hennesey 1979; Justice and Justice 1976; Stark et al. 1981). This is probably because behaviors that are considered to be illegitimate tend to be hidden. Detection of abusive actions can result in informal sanctions from friends, kin, and neighbors, and formal sanctions from police and the courts. Thus, all forms of family violence are likely to be less frequent in families that have friends or relatives who live nearby (Nye 1979). The presence of an active social support system may therefore deter elder abuse, because it is viewed as a highly illegitimate behavior. Phillips' case-control study found abused elderly persons more likely to be socially isolated.

Although it seems clear that these five factors are probable precipitants of elder abuse, it is important to realize that many of the relationships have not yet been established. Part 2 will focus on testing the relative importance of these risk factors.

PART TWO

Victims, Perpetrators, and Maltreatment

3

Characterizing Elder Abuse and Neglect: Who Are the Victims and the Perpetrators?

T HIS chapter presents the first in a series of analyses of the Model Project study data designed to add to our knowledge about the nature of elder abuse and neglect. A brief account of the development of the research instrument and the procedure for data collection is followed by a description of the victims and perpetrators in the study population and the types of mistreatment that were reported. Then, the relationship of the victim and perpetrator and their life situation are examined using the risk factors identified in the previous chapter as the framework for analysis.

We designed a case assessment form that was based in part on the Comprehensive Needs Assessment Procedure (CNAP) used by home care corporations in Massachusetts. The CNAP tool covered key demographic data about the victim, as well as information on physical and mental health, nutritional need, and social supports. Items specifically on elder abuse and neglect were added, including questions on the victim and perpetrator, manifestations and severity of abuse and neglect, actions taken, and the barriors to the delivery of services. The purpose of the case assessment was to provide a comprehensive picture of the abuse and neglect situation at the time that the case was referred to the agency, although in some instances it took several weeks for the social workers to gather the necessary information. To insure standardization of data, the assessments were conducted by site caseworkers, who had attended sev-

eral joint training sessions. All responses were monitored by the evaluation team. The forms were coded by one data clerk, and the values checked
by a member of the team prior to computerization.

VICTIMS AND PERPETRATORS

Included in the study were all cases of elder abuse and neglect seen by
the Model Projects between July 1, 1981, and June 30, 1983. The victims were 60 years of age and over and living in a domestic setting. The
perpetrators were family members or persons with whom the victims had
significant relationships. Specifically excluded were individuals living in
institutions and victims of self-neglect or crime by strangers. In total, there
were 328 substantiated cases (Worcester, 59; Syracuse, 135; and Rhode
Island, 134).[1]

At the time of the assessment, the average age of the victims was 76
years; 81 percent were female; 90 percent were white. About one-third
of the cases involved elders who were married and living with their spouses;
slightly more resided with children. The annual income for more than
half of the cases was under $5,000 a year. Even when the income of oth-
ers in the household was included, about half of the sample had earnings
of less than $10,000 annually. (See table 3.1.)

Of the perpetrators, 64 percent were male; 90 percent were white. Although 11 percent were 80 years or over, the majority were under 60 years
of age. Most often, the perpetrators were sons (in a quarter of the cases).
Daughters and husbands each represented a little less than one-fifth of
the perpetrators; other kin and nonrelatives, about one-eighth; and wives,
siblings, and in-laws even smaller proportions. On the average, the victim and the perpetrator had been living in the same household for a period of more than twenty years. (See table 3.2.)

1. Prior to pooling the data from the Model Projects, we compared the individual site samples on selected sociodemographic, health and functional status measures. No differences among
the three groups of victims were found for important independent variables including age, sex,
marital status, and living arrangements and for use of supportive devices or weight change (the
latter two items served as proxies for functional health). The perpetrators were alike in terms of
sex, living arrangements, history of mental illness, and alcoholism, although they differed somewhat in age (the Rhode Island sample had a significantly larger percentage of perpetrators under
50). Because of the overall similarity of the cases, we combined the samples from the three sites.
This larger number of cases enabled us to carry out subgroup analyses that would not have been
possible with a sample of 59 (Worcester) or even 134 (Rhode Island) or 135 (Syracuse).

TABLE 3.1: Sociodemographic characteristics of the victims

	#	%	N
Age			
60–64	53	16	
65–74	88	27	
75–84	119	36	
85 and older	63	20	
Average age = 76 years			
			(323)
Sex			
Female	268	82	
Male	60	18	
			(328)
Race			
White	295	90	
Black	19	6	
Native American	6	2	
Asian	3	1	
Latino	2	1	
Other	2	1	
			(327)
Marital status			
Widowed	159	50	
Married	100	32	
Divorced/separated	32	10	
Single	25	8	
			(316)
Living arrangements			
Lives alone	76	23	
With spouse	97	30	
With children	127	39	
With siblings	16	5	
With other relatives	58	18	
With nonrelatives	37	11	
			(326)[a]
Annual income of victims (1982)			
$ 4,999 or less	139	58	
5,000 to 9,999	77	32	
10,000 to 14,999	21	9	
15,000 and over	4	2	
			(241)

[a]Column adds up to more than 100 percent because of multiple responses.

TYPES OF ABUSE AND NEGLECT

Of the five types of mistreatment under investigation, psychological abuse was the most prevalent, occurring in almost three quarters of the cases.

TABLE 3.2: Sociodemographic characteristics of the perpetrator and relationship to victim

	#	%	N
Age			
39 and younger	86	28	
40–59	98	32	
60–79	90	29	
80 and older	33	11	
			(307)
Sex			
Male	204	64	
Female	115	36	
			(319)
Race			
White	287	90	
Black	21	7	
Native American	4	1	
Latino	2	1	
Asian	1	—	
Other	4	1	
			(319)
Relationship of perpetrator to victim[a]			
Son	92	28	
Daughter	60	18	
Husband	58	18	
Non-relative	45	14	
Other relatives	37	11	
Wife	22	7	
Sibling	17	5	
In-laws	14	4	
			(325)[a]
Perpetrator lives with victim			
Yes	240	75	
No	79	25	
			(319)

[a]Column adds up to more than 100 percent because of multiple responses.

The next most common type was physical abuse, identified in almost half the cases. Material abuse and passive neglect were each present in about one-third of the cases, and active neglect in one fifth. (See table 3.3.) On the average, two forms of maltreatment were reported for each victim, one of which was usually psychological abuse. When the caseworkers were asked which type of abuse in each case was responsible for the referral, psychological abuse was listed most often, followed in order by physical abuse, passive neglect, material abuse, and active neglect. Caseworkers were also requested to note which type of abuse they believed was most harmful to the victim. They cited physical abuse most frequently, followed by psychological abuse. In general, the mistreatment was not an isolated event but had occurred over a period of time that ranged from one month to 50 years, with a median of 12 months.

We also sought information about the manifestations of abuse and neglect and their severity (mild, moderate, severe, or intensity unknown).

TABLE 3.3: Types of abuse and neglect and severity

	#	%	N
Types reported			
Psychological abuse	236	72	
Physical abuse	150	46	
Material abuse	118	36	
Passive neglect	117	36	
Active neglect	65	20	
			(328)[a]
Types responsible for the referral			
Psychological abuse	142	43	
Physical abuse	126	38	
Passive neglect	82	25	
Material abuse	79	24	
Active neglect	46	14	
			(328)[a]
Types considered most harmful			
Physical abuse	115	35	
Psychological abuse	104	32	
Passive neglect	83	25	
Active neglect	50	15	
Material abuse	44	13	
			(328)[a]

[a]Columns add up to more than 100 percent because of multiple responses.

(See table 3.4.) Bruises and welts were the most common manifestations of physical abuse, present in 22 percent of the cases with about two-thirds of these judged to be of moderate or severe intensity. Other manifestations of physical violence (e.g., wounds, sexual molestation, etc.) were recorded in only a few cases. Evidence of intimidation, verbal assault, and humiliation were the most often documented forms of psychological abuse. They occurred with moderate or severe intensity in more than half of the cases. The most prevalent type of neglect was lack of support or companionship identified in slightly less than half the cases and almost always in moderate or severe degree of intensity. Material abuse was more likely to be "misuse of money or property," rather than "taking possession of money or property" with a large proportion of these acts considered to be in the moderate or severe categories. (See table 3.5.) For about half the victims, the situations were considered to be "life threatening" or "very threatening"; for most of the others, it was "moderately threatening." The evidence from the Model Projects, then, indicates that the maltreatment

TABLE 3.4: Manifestations of physical and psychological abuse

	#	%	N
Physical abuse			
Bruises, welts	69	22	
Direct beatings	30	9	
Physical confinement	30	9	
Malnutrition	14	4	
Sprains, dislocations	13	4	
Abrasions, lacerations	13	4	
Bone fractures	10	3	
Burns, scalding	10	3	
Wounds, cuts, punctures	5	2	
Sexual molestation	3	1	
Other manifestations	61	19	
			(316)
Psychological abuse			
Intimidation	175	59	(293)
Verbal assault	170	58	(294)
Humiliation	146	51	(286)
Threats	138	47	(293)
Isolation	130	6	(286)
Other manifestations	25	9	(275)

TABLE 3.5: Manifestations of material abuse and neglect

	#	%	N
Material abuse			
Misuse of money or property	99	40	(245)
Taking possession of money or property	82	33	(248)
Other (e.g., nonpayment of rent, etc.)	23	10	(240)
Neglect			
Lack of support or companionship	120	46	
Lack of supervision	99	37	
Lack of personal care	99	37	
Lack of food	93	35	
Lack of housekeeping help	66	25	
Failure to provide medical services	62	26	
Failure to purchase prescribed Rx	35	13	
Abandoned	25	10	
Lack of heat	24	9	
Failure to provide false teeth	17	7	
Failure to provide eyeglasses	15	6	
Failure to provide hearing aid	8	3	
Failure to fulfill other caretaking obligations (e.g., no furniture, etc.)	94	27	
			(264)

experienced by these elders was not trivial. Indeed, the major proportion of persons seen by the projects had been subjected to two or more types of abuse or neglect, and the effects tended to be quite serious.

RISK FACTOR DATA

Intra-individual dynamics

Since the psychological status of the perpetrator had been identified as a risk factor in the literature review, we added several questions to the assessment form to obtain information about mental status, alcohol and drug abuse, and provocative behavior. (See table 3.6.) Approximately two out of five perpetrators were reported to have a history of mental illness. The same proportion was found to abuse alcohol, to have experienced a recent decline in mental health status, and to have behaved more provoc-

TABLE 3.6: Psychological status of the perpetrators

	#	%	N
Recent decline in mental status	137	43	(317)
History of alcohol abuse	122	41	(301)
Provocative behavior toward the victim	126	40	(315)
History of mental illness	115	38	(301)
History of drug abuse	38	13	(301)

atively in behavior towards the victim than in the past. The proportion of drug abusers in the group was much smaller (one in eight).

Integenerational transmission of violent behavior

Even though the social workers spent many weeks and often months on the cases, gathering information about possible childhood maltreatment proved to be a difficult assignment. Responses to a question dealing with the childhood experiences of the perpetrator were only obtained in 75 of the 328 cases. Thirty-two of them reported that the perpetrator had been abused or neglected as a child. When the question was rephrased to determine if the perpetrator had come from an unstable or nontraditional family background, answers were furnished for 102 cases, 20 of which noted "violence."

Dependency

To ascertain the role of dependency as a risk factor in abuse and neglect situations, we included two sets of questions: one asked about functional status of the victims; the other, about the degree of dependency of the elder in performing tasks of daily living. (See table 3.7.) Almost half of the victims used a cane, walker, or wheelchair. Six percent were bedridden. In addition, the caseworkers noted that three out of four victims had experienced a recent decline in physical health. To determine the dependency status of the elderly clients, the caseworkers checked if the victims had problems with performance of activities of daily living (personal care, mobility and communication, mealtime activities, security of personal

property, management of financial and personal affairs, general shopping, transportation, and household management). For most victims,
problems were noted in almost all areas, ranging from transportation and
general shopping in three-quarters of the cases to security of property in
about three-fifths.

Problems with orientation were found in about two-fifths of the cases,
with a similar proportion exhibiting memory deficits. In response to questions about the abused person's emotional state prior to admission, the
social workers indicated that a majority (70 percent) were in a "poor"

TABLE 3.7: Functional/dependency status of the victims

	#	%	N
Problems with the instrumental activities of daily living			
Transportation	244	76	(322)
General shopping	241	75	(322)
Household management	236	73	(323)
Financial management	232	73	(321)
Mealtime activities	233	72	(323)
Mobility/communication	226	70	(322)
Personal care	223	69	(322)
Security of personal property	200	63	(317)
Problems with orientation all or some of the time			
Person	117	43	(274)
Place	106	34	(275)
Time	124	45	(273)
Problems with memory all or some of the time			
Immediate	119	44	(266)
Recent	127	48	(263)
Remote	108	43	(250)
Dependencies (very or slightly dependent)			
Companionship	261	84	(312)
Maintenance of property	203	74	(275)
Daily needs	216	70	(310)
Transportation	191	66	(288)
Financial management	199	65	(305)
Financial resources	88	30	(295)
Recent overall increase in dependency of victim on perpetrator	222	69	(324)

state. Forty-five percent were found to have had a recent decline in mental status at the time of admission into the project. On the other hand, over four-fifths were judged competent to give consent.

Another set of questions examined the dependency issue more directly. The victims were rated in six different areas (companionship, daily needs, financial management, financial resources, maintenance of property and transportation) with regard to the extent of their dependency on the abuser (very dependent, slightly dependent, independent). Among the cases in the sample, the highest proportion of dependency was associated with companionship: 84 percent of the victims were either very or slightly dependent. The next highest area of dependence was "maintenance of property," followed in order by "daily needs," "transportation," "financial management," and "financial resources." Overall, a recent increase in dependency was recorded for more than two-thirds of the cases.

Collecting information about the perpetrators to determine their dependency on the victims (finances, companionship, activities of daily living, and other) was more difficult. The data on financial dependency were available on three quarters of the sample, but there were not enough responses to the other items (daily needs, companionship) for meaningful results. In contrast to the victims, 70 percent of whom were *independent* of the abuser and/or family members for financial resources, a similar proportion of the perpetrators (68 percent) were very or slightly *dependent* on the victim for economic support. A recent increase in overall dependency of the perpetrators was reported to have occurred in 22 percent of the cases.

External stress

To learn more about the role of external stress—that is, stress resulting from factors outside of the family—as a causal factor in cases of elderly mistreatment, we requested the case workers to record whether certain events (see table 3.8) had occurred in the lives of the perpetrators. Of the listed conditions, the most common ones in the caseloads were "long term financial difficulties" and "recent changes in living arrangements," identified in one-third of the cases; next, were "long-term" and "recent medical complaints" and "recent financial problems" associated with about one-quarter of the perpetrators. Other problems affected less than one-tenth of the cases.

TABLE 3.8: Stressful events in the lives of the perpetrators

	#	%	N
Long-term financial problems	101	34	
Recent change in living arrangements	100	32	
Long-term medial complaint	79	26	
Recent financial problems	73	24	
Recent medical complaint	73	24	
Recent divorce or separation	45	15	
Recent death of spouse or significant other	24	8	
Recent birth of child	3	1	
			(301)

Social isolation

Several questions on the case assessment form sought to determine the amount of social contact of the victims: the total number of social contacts for the victims (except for those involving the perpetrator and formal caregivers), the frequency with which they saw these people (daily, weekly, or monthly or infrequently) and whether they attended clubs, senior center activities, or church on a regular basis. (See table 3.9.) The results showed that about one in five victims had no social contact other than with the perpetrator, whereas about one in ten had five or more contacts. For almost one-quarter of the sample, the contact was on a daily basis. Only a very small proportion had been attending club or church programs. With regard to the social contacts and networks of the perpetrators, the information was more limited. (See table 3.10.) About three-quarters of the perpetrators had family members available for support or assistance and more than nine-tenths had someone to call on in a crisis.

SUMMARY

From the data collected in the case assessment process, a picture of the Model Project victims, perpetrators and abuse and neglect situations begins to emerge. The victims averaged 76 years in age. They were more likely to be female than male and to be living in households with spouses and/or other family members. The perpetrators tended to be sons rather than husbands, wives, or daughters. Psychological abuse appeared to be the most common type, but usually accompanied by other forms. An analysis of the manifestations of abuse indicated that physical abuse was most often characterized by bruises and welts; psychological abuse, by verbal assault and intimidation; and neglect by lack of support and companionship. For a sizable proportion of victims in all sites, the situation was considered by project staff to be very threatening or life-threatening.

Generally, the victims were somewhat functionally impaired. About half required supportive devices for mobility; a few were bedridden. A large majority had difficulties with some activities of daily living and were assessed to be in a poor emotional state. Cognitive impairment was found

TABLE 3.9: Social network of the victim

	#	%	N
Number of persons with whom victim has social contact			
None	68	21	
One	66	21	
Two	68	21	
Three	52	16	
Four	29	9	
Five or more	36	11	
			(319)
Frequency of contacts			
Daily	76	26	
Weekly	102	35	
Monthly/infrequently	48	16	
None	68	23	
			(294)
Victim attends club/church activities			
Yes	21	7	
No	279	93	
			(300)
Victim has someone to call in a crisis			
Yes	236	83	
No	50	17	
			(286)
Victim has experienced a recent loss of supports/contacts			
Yes	131	40	
No	193	60	
			(324)

in almost one-half of the caseload, although a great majority of the victims were considered to be "legally competent" to give consent. Notwithstanding the fact that this group was dependent on their caregivers or other family members for daily needs, financial management, transportation and companionship, they were relatively independent in terms of financial resources. For many victims, the perpetrators (and, at times, formal caregivers), were their only social contact.

The perpetrators were more likely to be dependent on the victims for finances, but independent in other ways. Their lives were stressful. Health and financial problems troubled them. One-third were said to have had psychological problems and an even larger proportion, a history of mental illness and alcohol abuse. These individuals tended to have unrealistic expectations of the capability of the abused elders and to view their demands for attention as unreasonable. For a majority of the group, it was not possible to learn whether family violence was present in their earlier history.

Case examples

Two case example are presented below to illustrate more dramatically the relationship of the risk factors to elder abuse and neglect that was expressed statistically in the previous pages.

TABLE 3.10: Social network of the perpetrator

	#	%	N
Family member available for support			
Yes	178	76	
No	57	24	
			(235)
Someone is available in a crisis			
Yes	201	93	
No	16	7	
			(217)
Perpetrator has experienced a recent loss of supports/contacts			
Yes	89	28	
No	227	72	
			(316)

Case 1

Frances was an 88-year-old widow who lived in her own single-family home in a pleasant, middle-class neighborhood. George, her 55-year-old son, had lived with his mother all his life. He lost his job five years ago and had a reputation as a heavy drinker.

When the model project received a report from a clergyman that Frances had been abused by her son, the worker arranged to accompany the clergyman on a visit the next day. Frances' house was attractive enough from the exterior, but the inside was another matter. It was dark, shabby, grimy, and obviously had not received much care in years. Frances was unkempt, her dress ragged, and she clearly had not bathed for some time. Her vision was poor, one eye was bothering her, and she was hard of hearing. Her legs were swollen and badly bruised, and there were lacerations on one foot, which were infected. However, despite her problems, she seemed bright and cheerful.

Reluctantly, she confessed that her son had thrown a cooking implement at her a few days before, when she burned some food. She also conceded that this was not the first such incident.

It became evident that neglect was an even larger issue than abuse. Frances had not seen a doctor for years, her nutrition was poor, she had no decent clothes or shoes. She seemed to sincerely believe that she was poor, but the worker discovered that she had over $50,000 in the bank, the appreciation on an inheritance earmarked for a "rainy day." An elderly in-law dropped by periodically to cash her Social Security checks, pay her bills, and give her the remaining cash, which she kept in her pocketbook and doled out to her son.

In many ways, this case can be considered fairly typical of the physical abuse cases which make up half of the study population, especially those in which the perpetrator is a son. The adult child is financially dependent on the parent and is an alcohol abuser. Little mention in the case history is made of the psychological state of the perpetrator, but substance abuse, which has been found to be related to family violence, may be a symptom of emotional problems. The son appears to be unable to cope with life, to hold a job, or to be independent of his mother. Although she has a need for some assistance in her daily activities, she cannot depend on her son to fulfill the role of caregiver. Rather than anger and violence arising from the stress of caregiving, the conflict in this family is rooted in the dependency relationship of the abuser on his victim.

She provides a home for him and takes care of his other financial needs. His reaction may be due to his lack of power in a situation in which his aged mother still exercises control.

The importance of the other risk factors to this case history is less evident. There are not enough data to know if the perpetrator grew up in an abusive household or if his financial situation was a matter of great stress to him. It does not appear that the family was socially isolated, for there was some contact with other family members.

Another case example is given below. This one concerns financial exploitation and physical abuse.

Case 2

Elsie and William, age 90 and 83, were sister and brother. They lived in a run-down tenement in the inner city and shared an apartment with George, a 60-year old boarder. Elsie had been a widow for some time. She was thin and wraith-like, but her appearance was deceptive; she is a "survivor." Elsie felt responsible for her brother, the "baby" of a once large family. William, who had never married, appeared quiet and reclusive. He had a hearing problem and spent much of his time reading.

One Friday afternoon, a report was received that Elsie has been physically abused by the boarder, George, and had been locked out of her apartment. She had taken refuge with a neighbor who had called the police. William reportedly had been frightened by the disturbance and had "gone for a walk."

The elder abuse worker called the visiting nurse association for assistance and met the assigned nurse at the neighbor's apartment. An examination of Elsie revealed no evidence of physical abuse, but she was believed to be in a weakened condition, possibly the result of poor nutrition. The neighbor reported that the police had come, but by the time they arrived, George had left. She said that she had heard Elsie being beaten on a number of occasions when George had come home drunk. She also suspected that George was taking money from Elsie and her brother. The police had been called a number of times, but had been frustrated when Elsie would not swear out a complaint.

In later visits, Elsie let an elder abuse worker and an outreach worker in, but she still refused offers of assistance. William, on the other hand, began to open up. Despite the problems in communicating with him, he let the workers know that he was not happy with what was going on and planned to move out. Neighbors approached the workers to report further instances of abuse by George. They described him as an alcoholic and a gambler who took money from Elsie and William and spent it at the track. Elsie and George had been drinking for years. She would go from one agency to another to obtain food, then sell it, and hand the proceeds over to George.

The dynamics within this household are somewhat different from those in Case 1. The perpetrator is not a member of the family but apparently has a significant relationship to the sister, who is reluctant to take legal action against him. The brother appears to be an innocent victim in this situation. No other information is available about the perpetrator, except that he is a gambler and drinker. The sister seems to be emotionally dependent on him. He in turn is dependent on her for money. Again, with limited information about the abuse, or only hearsay, it is difficult to determine if certain stressful events triggered the abuse or if it is a repeated pattern of violence learned in childhood. Social isolation does not appear to be a factor, except perhaps for the brother.

In later chapters, we examine how the Model Projects handled these types of cases. For now, it seems clear from both the general description of the study population and the case examples that among the risk factors, intra-individual dynamics and dependency are particularly important predictors of elder mistreatment. The relationship of stressful life events and social isolation is less obvious, but does seem to be influential in some of the cases. Information on the intergenerational transmission of abuse was available for so few cases that its role in elder abuse was impossible to substantiate.

4

Variations in Elder Maltreatment

T HE objective of the two analyses described in this chapter is to examine the relationship of the risk factors to elder abuse and neglect. The first was a comparative analysis of the five discrete categories of abuse and neglect (physical, psychological, and material abuse; active and passive neglect) using the variables described in the previous chapter. This approach is particularly relevant in light of the comments made by Pedrick-Cornell and Gelles (1981:459) who, after reviewing the literature in the field, criticized the early researchers for lumping together various types of abuse or neglect. Acts of *commission*, they wrote, must be seen as conceptually distinct from acts of *omission*. Violence, for example, must be viewed as different in kind and cause from neglect.

The second analysis was a comparison of cases by type of perpetrator, but limited to spouses (spouse abuse) and adult children (parent abuse). Although the early research on elder abuse revealed that a substantial proportion of elder abusers were spouses, no effort was ever made to differentiate this group of cases from those that involved other relatives within the household. Furthermore, researchers on spouse abuse did not address the issue of older couples who often were part of their samples. It is likely,

This chapter was co-authored by Michael A. Godkin. The contents on the comparison of types of abuse appeared in slightly altered form in Rosalie S. Wolf, Michael A. Godkin, and Karl A. Pillemer (1986). "Maltreatment of the Elderly: A Comparative Analysis." *Pride Institute Journal of Long-Term Home Health Care.* 5(4):10–17.

however, that the dynamics between spouses and between parent and adult child are quite different, and that including the two groups of perpetrators in one sample could confound the results. Thus, this analysis was viewed as important in clarifying some of the conflicting findings in earlier research.

COMPARISON OF TYPES OF ELDER MALTREATMENT

Since it was not possible to conduct this case comparison using mutually exclusive categories (of the 328 cases, only 88 were victims of just one type of abuse or neglect), contingency tables were constructed comparing cases on the variables under study in which one type of maltreatment was present or absent: that is, cases with one type of abuse were contrasted with the rest of the sample that did not include that particular form of mistreatment. For each of the five categories of mistreatment and variables mentioned above, we generated a set of cross-tabulations. Although this method could not identify factors based on mutually exclusive categories, it could show the characteristics more likely to be associated with one type of abuse or neglect than with others. Only, significant differences (chi square, $p \leq .05$) found in the cross-tabulations are described below and summarized in table 4.1.

Characteristics of victims and perpetrators

In the analysis of the types of mistreatment by the sociodemographic variables, there were significant differences among the various types of abuse and neglect for victim's age, marital status and living arrangements (but not for sex, race or income). In general, the elders who were physically abused tended to be younger, married, and living with others. On the other hand, elders who were neglected (unintentionally) were more likely to be older and not married. Victims of material abuse tended to be single, widowed, or divorced but, unlike physically or psychologically abused elders, to be living alone.

Age also differed among the perpetrators, with those involved in material exploitation usually younger than the perpetrators of other forms of abuse or neglect. Not surprisingly, the living arrangement of the perpetrator was a significant factor, with those reported to have physically or psychologically abused an elder usually sharing living quarters with the victim in contrast to perpetrators of material exploitation who were less likely to live with their victims.

The cross-tabulation of type of maltreatment and victim–perpetrator relationship (husband, wife, son, daughter, sibling, other relatives and non-relatives) produced significant results for physical, psychological, and material abuse. Whereas both physical and psychological abuse were associated with those cases in which the abuser was a spouse, rather than another relative or nonrelative, the reverse was true in cases of material abuse.

Risk factor data

Intra-individual dynamics. Both physical and psychological abuse appear to be associated with perpetrators who have had psychological problems as defined in the study. Among those perpetrators who had experienced a decline in mental health, the proportion of physical and psychological abuse was greater than among those whose mental state had been stable. Another measure employed to characterize the mental status of the perpetrator, "history of mental illness," was a significant factor again for physical and psychological abuse, with higher proportions of physical and psychological abusers among the perpetrators who had a history of mental illness than those with no history. On the other hand, active neglect was less likely to be associated with mental illness.

A similar pattern of relationships existed between type of mistreatment and "the perpetrator's unrealistic expectations of the victim." Of those cases in which the perpetrators had unrealistic expectations of the victim, more involved psychological abuse than those in which the perpetrators had realistic expectations. For passive neglect, the relationship was reversed. More cases of passive neglect involved perpetrators with realistic expectations. One final variable in this group, alcohol abuse, was significantly related to physical and material abuse. A larger proportion of perpetrators with alcohol problems were involved with physical and material abuse than the perpetrators who had no problem.

Dependency

Physical status of the victim. Two questions on the assessment form were used to determine the physical status of the victims. They were:

TABLE 4.1: Profiles of victims and perpetrators according to

	Physical Abuse	Psychological Abuse
VICTIM		
SOCIODEMOGRAPHICS		
Age/Marital Status	Younger married	
DEPENDENCY		
Physical/Functional Status	More independent in IADL/ADL	More independent in IADL/ADL
Psychological/ Cognitive Status	Poor emotional health	Poor emotional health; oriented in 3 spheres; no recent decline in mental status
SOCIAL NETWORK	Stable	Emergency contact available
PERPETRATOR		
SOCIODEMOGRAPHICS Age/Sex		
Living Arrangements	Lives with victim	Lives with victim
PSYCHOLOGICAL STATUS	History of mental illness; alcohol abuse; recent decline in mental status	History of mental illness; recent decline in mental status; unrealistic expectation of victim
DEPENDENCY		
Physical Status	Recent decline in health	Recent and long-term medical complaints
Dependency Issues	Increased dependency	
Quality of Relationship to Victim		
STRESS	No recent financial problems	
SOCIAL NETWORK		

type of maltreatment (only significant relationships shown)

Material Abuse	Active Neglect	Passive Neglect
Not married		Older/not married
Problems with finance mgt. and transportation	Problems with IADL; dependent for ADL and companionship; need for supportive devices	Problems with IADL; need for supportive devices; dependent in ADL and companionship
	Problems with orientation and memory	Recent decline in mental health; problems with orientation, memory and giving consent
Recent loss of supports	No emergency contact	Loss of social supports
Younger Does not live with victim	Older/Female	
Alcohol abuse; no recent decline in mental status	No history of mental illness	Realistic expectations
No recent medical complaints		Recent medical complaint
Financial dependency	No change in dependency	No financial dependency
	Victim is a source of stress	Victim is a source of stress
Recent change in financial/job status; long-term and recent financial problems		
No family available for support		Loss of social supports

"change in physical health status" and "use of supportive devices," both of which produced significant results when cross-tabulated with the various types of mistreatment. Four times as many active neglect cases and twice as many passive neglect cases were identified with victims who had experienced a recent decline in physical health than those whose health was stable. Similar findings were obtained for "supportive devices." Among the victims using supportive devices, active and passive neglect occurred more than twice as often than among victims who did not need these aids. On the basis of this initial investigation into the relationship between dependency and type of mistreatment, it appeared that the victims of neglect were likely to be in poorer health than old people who were physically or psychologically abused.

Instrumental activities of daily living. Generally, elders who had a higher degree of functioning were more likely to be victims of physical and psychological abuse, whereas those with problems performing instrumental activities were more apt to be victims of neglect. Eight activities were significant in the analysis: personal care, mobility, meal preparation, security of property, financial management, general shopping, transportation, and household management. The rate of physical and psychological abuse was less among victims with problems in the above activities than those with no difficulties. On the other hand, the proportions of active and passive neglect were many times greater. Security/safety of property was the only activity that was significantly related to material abuse. Financial exploitation was more apt to occur in those cases in which there was a problem with security than those in which no problem was cited.

Psychological and cognitive function of the victim. The three measures used to determine cognitive function (orientation, memory and ability to give consent) produced significant results for all types of maltreatment, except material abuse. Again, abuse was associated with a higher level of functioning and neglect with a greater degree of impairment. Psychological abuse and passive neglect were significant factors for all categories of orientation (person, place, time) and memory (immediate, recent, and remote). A similar pattern was found for physical abuse and active neglect but limited to selective aspects of orientation and memory. Physical abuse was negatively related to orientation to place and to immediate and remote memory. Active neglect was a significant factor for all three spheres of orientation and immediate memory as well. It was twice as likely to involve elders with these cognitive problems than those who did not have them. The last factor, ability to give consent, was significant for psychological abuse and active and passive neglect. Again, the pattern was repeated, with psychological abuse more frequently associated with victims who were able to give consent than with those who were deemed incompetent. Conversely, active and passive neglect were found more often in cases of incompetency than competency.

No matter which factor representing functional state was used in the analysis, the results were similar. Among the cases in this study, the most impaired victims were those who had been neglected, either passively or actively; the most intact victims, physically as well as cognitively, were those who had been abused physically or psychologically. No differentiation with regard to functional status could be made for victims of material abuse, except in the area of security of property.

Dependency status of the victim. In each of the six specific dependency areas investigated—financial resources, financial management, companionship, transportation, daily needs, and property maintenance—there were significant relationships with one or more types of mistreatment. For the physical abuse cases, the significant factors were companionship and daily needs, with more physical abuse cases associated with victims who were independent than dependent. Psychological abuse was related to all of the dependencies listed above (except financial resources), in the same direction.

All six dependency areas were significant for active neglect, with six times as many neglect cases found in the group of victims who were "very dependent" than in the group who were "independent." Likewise, passive neglect was more likely related to those cases in which the victims were "very dependent" (except for financial resources, which was not significant).

In addition to the specific dependency areas, the study also examined the relationship of types of mistreatment to an "increase in dependency of the victim." Significant results were noted for all categories of maltreatment except material abuse. More cases of abuse were associated with victims who were reported to have experienced no increase in dependency than with victims who became more dependent. Conversely, a larger proportion of neglect cases was present among cases with increased dependency than among those that showed no change.

From the outcome of the preceding analysis, a pattern emerged which showed that victims of neglect, both intentional and unintentional, were more dependent on their caregivers than were the victims of physical and psychological abuse. This relationship not only existed for the various areas of dependency in the study but also for cases in which an increase in dependency was recorded. The dependency-abuse dynamic was further clar-

ified by examining the opposite configuration: the dependency of the perpetrator on the victim.

   Dependency status of the perpetrator. The cross-tabulation of health
status variables (selected to indicate dependency of the perpetrator) and
types of abuse produced a number of significant findings. Both physical
and material abuse were related to "decline in physical status," but in
opposite ways. Physical abuse was more often associated with perpetrators
who had experienced a decline in physical status than those whose health
had remained stable, whereas material abuse was more likely to be related
to perpetrators whose health status was unchanged. When analyzing type
of abuse by long-term medical complaints, the results were also mixed.
There was a higher proportion of perpetrators of psychological abuse with
long-term medical complaints compared to those without these problems. Other types of abuse and neglect showed no differences. For perpetrators who had recent medical complaints, two types of maltreatment
were significant. The percentage of perpetrators of psychological abuse
and passive neglect was higher for those with recent complaints than those
who were reported to have none. Again, the material abuse cases provided contrasting findings; a smaller proportion of material abusers complained of recent medical problems.

   Two other measures of perpetrator "dependency" also yielded significant results: one, "increase in dependency needs" was related to physical
abuse and active neglect; the other, "financial dependency" was related
to material abuse and passive neglect. More perpetrators of physical abuse
were in the increased dependency group than in the group where no change
in dependency had occurred, whereas perpetrators of active neglect were
more likely to be in the latter group. With regard to financial dependency, as might be expected, the rate of material abuse was highest for
those perpetrators who were perceived as very dependent on the victim
for financial resources and lowest for those who were financially independent. Again, the results for neglect (passive, in this instance) are the opposite of those for the abuse, with more perpetrators of passive neglect
financially independent of the victim.

   The contrasting relationship between the risk factors for abuse and neglect was also noted in the cross-tabulation of type of mistreatment and
the perpetrator's "perception of the victim as a source of stress." Among
those cases in which the stress was judged to be "a lot," the proportion
of material abuse was about one-half of what it was among those cases in
which no stress was noted. There were about five times as many active
neglect cases and twice as many passive neglect cases in the portion of

the sample that included "a lot of stress" than in the portion that recorded no stress.

Although the findings that related dependency of the perpetrator and type of mistreatment were not as extensive as those concerned with the victim, the evidence indicated that the dependency of the perpetrator was a significant factor for abuse and neglect. Physical and psychological abuse appeared to be related to declining health status of the perpetrator, and material abuse to financial needs whereas neglect was more likely to be associated with perpetrators in stable health, of independent means, but under greater stress.

External stress

Of the five stressful events examined (death of spouse or significant other; divorce or separation; recent change in living arrangements; recent change in job or financial status; and recent and long term financial problems), only the last three were significant, and they involved material abuse and/ or passive neglect. Both perpetrators of material abuse and passive neglect were more likely to have had a recent change in living arrangements and recent financial problems. In addition, more perpetrators who had experienced a change in job or financial status and who had long term financial problems were associated with material abuse than those who had no money troubles.

Social insolation

The analysis examined both the social network of the victim and the perpetrator. No distinctions could be made among the various types of maltreatment with regard to number and frequency of social contacts of the victims or their attendance at clubs and church events. However, a "recent loss of supports/contacts" by the victim occurred in physical and material abuse and passive neglect. Among the cases in which the victims had experienced a loss of supports, the proportion of physical abuse was lower, but higher for material abuse and passive neglect, than among those in which no losses were recorded.

A more direct question regarding the social network of the victim was whether the elder had someone to call in a crisis. Of those cases in which the victim had an emergency contact, the rate of psychological abuse was higher than those cases in which the victim had no emergency contact. Both types of neglect were more likely to be associated with cases in which there was no one to call in a crisis than those in which an emergency contact was available.

A "recent loss of supports" by the perpetrator was also related to passive neglect. More perpetrators who had experienced a recent loss of supports were involved in passive neglect than those whose support systems were intact. Similarly, among those cases in which there had been a change in the family relationships, the proportion of passive neglect was higher in contrast to cases in which no change had taken place. When the question was rephrased to ask whether family members were available for support, the results were significant for material abuse. Those perpetrators were less likely to have family support available.

Discussion

To a large extent, these comparative analyses were successful in identifying the differences among the categories. We must remember, however, that the comparisons were between cases in which a certain type of mistreatment was present and cases which involved one or more *other* types of mistreatment. Nevertheless, the results do permit us to make some general statements about each type.

Physical abuse is closely linked to the mental health of the perpetrator and to a lesser degree, to that of the victim. Both the victim and the perpetrator of physical abuse were found to be in poor emotional health. A significantly high proportion of perpetrators also had a history of mental illness, had suffered a recent decline in mental health, and had become increasingly provocative toward the victim. Factors related to the impairment and dependency status of the victim do not seem to be as important in these cases as in neglect. The victims of physical abuse were among the younger ones in the sample, had a higher level of cognitive functioning and greater ability to perform instrumental activities of daily living. Since physical abuse involved family members who were most intimately related and emotionally connected, it is likely that this form of mistreatment has its underpinnings in long-standing, pathological family dynamics and interpersonal processes that become more highly charged when the dependency relationship is altered, either because of illness or financial needs.

The psychologically abused elders were the least likely to be disabled, dependent or socially isolated. A majority were well oriented to person, place and time and had few problems with immediate, recent or remote memory. Yet, their emotional state was judged by the case workers to be "poor." The perpetrator of psychological abuse was likely to have had a history of mental illness and to have suffered a recent decline in mental health. In addition, they appeared to be plagued by both recent and long term medical complaints. Their poor mental and physical health status, coupled with unrealistic expectations of their victims, suggest that interpersonal dynamics may be a clue to the etiology of psychological abuse.

Material abuse seems to be best understood by focusing on the financial problems of the perpetrator and the relative vulnerability of the victim. A significantly higher percentage of material abuse occurred in cases where the perpetrators had a history of financial difficulties. Factors related to the physical and mental state of the victims appeared to be relatively unimportant in these cases. The finding that a significantly high proportion of material abuse involved distant relatives or parties who were unrelated by birth or marriage, and who did not live together, lends support to the idea that financial gain, rather than interpersonal pathology, is the most important issue in material abuse. Although alcohol abuse may be rather common among these perpetrators, unlike the perpetrators of physical or psychological abuse, they did not experience any recent decline in their mental state.

In marked contrast to the cases of physical or psychological abuse, those involving neglect appear to be related to the dependency needs of the victims. To the caregivers in these situations, the victims were seen as a source of stress. Because of impaired cognitive and physical functioning, these elders had to rely on their caregivers to assist them with a variety of daily activities, as well as to provide companionship. In cases of passive neglect, the victim's functional status appeared to be compromised further by a decline in mental health and loss of social supports. The perpetrators under these circumstances may be responding to their own medical problems or recent financial difficulties. Differences noted between active neglect and other forms of mistreatment seemed to center on the lack of mental or dependency problems on the part of the perpetrators, even though they were more likely to be older and female.

These findings suggest that there are distinct differences in the dynamics within the domestic setting that lead to mistreatment of elderly people. The profiles appear to be consistent and logical, but, of course, will need further testing. By approaching the data in this fashion, we have further evidence of the importance of psychological status of the perpetrator and dependency and exchange relations as risk factors. Again the role of social isolation and external stress factors is not so clearly indicated.

COMPARISON OF SPOUSE AND PARENT ABUSE

We also compared spousal and parent abuse cases on each of the study variables. Of the 328 perpetrators in the sample, 80 were spouses and 152 were adult children. (The remainder were other relatives or non-relatives.) The victims of abuse by spouses and adult children did not differ significantly on sex and age, but of course, there was a difference in marital status. All victims of spouse abuse were married but only one-sixth of those mistreated by adult children. Almost three quarters of those elderly persons mistreated by their children were widows.

When we examined the types of abuse, we found that physical maltreatment was more prevalent in cases of spouse abuse than in cases of parent abuse (table 4.2). On the other hand, material exploitation was more characteristic of parent abuse than spouse abuse. Although the proportion of psychological abuse did not significantly differ between the two groups, a comparison of the individual manifestations of psychological abuse showed that the severity of the problem was greater for victims of parent abuse than spouse abuse; that is, a greater proportion of victims of parent abuse endured "severe" manifestations of verbal assault, threats, intimidation, and humiliation than victims of spouse abuse. Similarly, the results showed that more of the cases involving adult children as perpetra-

TABLE 4.2: Types of mistreatment

	Spouse Abuse			Parent Abuse	
	#	%		#	%
Physical abuse					
Yes	47	64		68	46
No	26	36		81	54
$p = .0130$					
Material abuse					
Yes	8	11		54	36
No	67	89		94	64
$p = .0001$					

tors were assessed to be "life threatening" by the case workers than those in which spouses were the perpetrators (table 4.3).

When comparisons were made regarding the dependency status of the victims, a larger proportion of victims of spouse abuse were found to be dependent on their abusers for companionship, financial management, property maintenance and financial resources than those mistreated by their adult children (table 4.4). While there were no differences between the two groups of victims in functional ability, cognition, and health sta-

TABLE 4.3: Severity of manifestations of abuse

	Spouse Abuse		Parent Abuse	
	#	%	#	%
Verbal assault				
Mild	4	7	3	4
Moderate	30	52	19	26
Severe	24	41	52	70
$p = .0038$				
Threats				
Mild	2	5	5	8
Moderate	21	50	11	17
Severe	19	45	48	75
$p = .0015$				
Intimidation				
Mild	1	2	6	8
Moderate	28	56	23	29
Severe	21	42	49	63
$p = .0082$				
Humiliation				
Mild	4	9	6	9
Moderate	24	53	19	38
Severe	17	38	43	63
$p = .0193$				
Level of threat of all manifestations				
Life or very threatening	32	44	89	62
Moderate or not really threatening	41	56	55	38
$p = .0176$				

tus, a significantly larger percentage of the elders victimized by spouses were found to be in poor emotional health compared to those who were abused or neglected by their offspring.

There were also variations in the problems experienced by the two groups of abusers (table 4.5). More spouse abusers had both new and long-standing medical complaints or had undergone a recent deterioration in physical health status than the adult children. Conversely, a history of mental illness, alcohol abuse, and financial and job difficulties, both recent and long term, were more often associated with the adult children than the spouses. Some of them also had experienced a recent loss of spouse through divorce or separation (which, by definition, did not occur in the spouse group). Further evidence of stress in the lives of perpetrators, character-

TABLE 4.4: Dependency status of the victim

	Spouse Abuse		Parent Abuse	
	#	%	#	%
Financial resources				
Independent	23	32	110	85
Slightly dependent	22	31	9	7
Very dependent	27	38	10	8
$p = .0000$				
Financial management				
Independent	15	20	56	40
Slightly dependent	10	14	12	9
Very dependent	49	66	71	51
$p = .0311$				
Companionship				
Independent	6	8	24	17
Slightly dependent	6	8	23	16
Very dependent	63	84	97	67
$p = .0311$				
Maintenance of property				
Independent	9	13	40	31
Slightly dependent	13	19	17	13
Very dependent	48	69	71	56
$p = .0157$				

ized by a change in living arrangements, was also more frequently associated with the adult offspring than the spouses (table 4.6). Finally, of the variables employed to test for social isolation, only the number of social contacts was significant; twice as many cases of parent abuse were without social contacts than those involving spouses.

Case examples

Because so little attention has been given to the topic of spouse abuse among the elderly, several cases from the Model Projects files are summarized below as examples of marital conflict in the aging family.

TABLE 4.5: Physical and mental health problems of the perpetrators

	Spouse Abuse		Parent Abuse	
	#	%	#	%
Recent medical complaint				
Yes	30	40	25	17
No	45	60	120	83
$p = .0040$				
Long-term medical complaint				
Yes	33	44	30	21
No	45	56	115	79
$p = .0050$				
Change in physical health				
Yes	47	64	30	21
No	27	37	116	79
$p = .0000$				
History of mental illness				
Yes	24	29	70	48
No	53	71	75	52
$p = .0106$				
History of alcohol abuse				
Yes	24	32	70	48
No	51	68	75	52
$p = .0300$				

Case 1

Mr. and Mrs. B were a couple in their sixties who had been married for forty years, separated only for a six-month period, twenty years earlier, when the husband was hospitalized in a psychiatric facility, following an industrial accident that resulted in temporary memory loss. Since that time, he has been unable to work, suffering from severe emphysema and a heart condition. Until eleven months prior to the referral of the case to the Elder Abuse Project, his wife was his active caretaker. She then suffered a stroke which left her with paralysis on her right side and a heart condition, unable to am-

TABLE 4.6: Stressful events in the lives of the perpetrators

	Spouse Abuse		Parent Abuse	
	#	%	#	%
Recent financial problems				
Yes	11	15	41	28
No	64	85	105	72
$p = .0395$				
Long-term financial problems				
Yes	9	12	59	41
No	66	88	86	59
$p = .0000$				
Change in financial/job status				
Yes	18	24	63	43
No	56	76	83	57
$p = .0097$				
Loss of spouse through separation or divorce				
Yes	—	—	34	23
No	75	100	111	77
$p = .0000$				
Change in living arrangements				
Yes	18	24	58	40
No	58	76	88	60
$p = .0250$				

bulate, toilet, dress, or transfer herself independently. Following a short convalescent period in a nursing facility, her husband took her home against the doctor's wishes. A home health agency was called to provide skilled nursing and home health services. The visiting nurse made the referral to the Elder Abuse Project.

Because of her deteriorated physical condition, Mrs. B was no longer able to care for her husband or her home. Mr. B felt that he must pay her back for her care of him by assuming caregiving responsibilities, but they were difficult for him both physically and psychologically. He could not accept the fact that his wife would not walk again nor the emotional changes that seemed to have occurred as a result of the stroke. He was very dependent on his wife for companionship. Mrs. B said that her husband was "punishing" her. Mr. B told the nurse that he felt like hitting his wife with a baseball bat— but didn't. Evidence of maltreatment documented in the case included bruises, verbal assault, threats, and failure to properly care for his wife.

Case 2

Physical and psychological abuse of Mrs. K by her husband had been present during most of the fifty-four years of their marriage. She suffered from mental and physical problems, including diabetes, hyperthyroidism, hypertension, and visual impairment. For a time, a decade earlier, she was taken in by a sister-in-law because of her inability to cook and keep house, a problem related to her poor vision. Mr. K functioned well enough as a soldier during the war and as a machinist thereafter, but had been an alcoholic for years. Both Mr. and Mrs. K had relatives who took care of their finances and shopping because of their lack of competence. His maltreatment of his wife reflected a number of things: a family pattern of violence; the fact that his wife was never able to function as a housekeeper; and his feelings that the once attractive woman he married was now "grotesque," and "half-blind." He rarely appeared to be completely sober, but despite everything did not seem unhappy. He was very dependent on his wife for companionship. Her deteriorating condition and increased dependency led to a crisis and a referral to the Elder Abuse Project.

Case 3

Mr. A, 82 years old, first came to the attention of the Elder Abuse Project when he was to leave the hospital, at which time it was learned that he had no home to return to. His wife of forty-five years saw his latest hospitalization as an opportunity to escape from a situation that she found more and more difficult. Aided by a favorite son, she took most of the furniture and money and moved in with her son in another state. Fifteen years younger than her husband, Mrs. A had been the breadwinner of the family long after her husband had reached retirement age. He had been an outdoorsman, and a "free spirit"; she did not share his interests. He had one favorite son; she, another. He suffered from a variety of physical ailments; needed oxygen; had limited mobility, hearing and vision; and a history of mental illness. Dependent on his wife financially and for companionship, transportation, daily needs, and maintenance of property, he wanted her back, but had unrealistic expectations of her ability to respond to his needs. Psychological abuse, material exploitation, and active neglect were the manifestations of mistreatment recorded in the case.

What do these cases have in common? The long-term medical complaints, recent decline in health, poor emotional state, increased dependency, and, in some instances, history of mental illness and alcoholism provide a context within the marital relationship in which anger, hostility, and abuse can more easily erupt. For some couples, such as those above, the stresses of later life, particularly declining health, can exacerbate an already tension-filled and unhappy marriage. Johnson (1985) reports that even among caregivers who express satisfaction with their marriages, there is evidence of underlying anger. Many people who are locked into unhappy marriages cannot cope with the increased demands that illness brings especially when they themselves may also be in failing health (Zarit, Todd, and Zarit 1986). In Finkelhor and Pillemer's (1987) case-control study, a high degree of marital conflict was associated with abuse.

Guilford (1986) has described unhappy marriages of later life as those in which there are diminished feelings of marital intimacy, lack of mutual interests, differing values, inability to express true feelings, and frequent disagreements. Although some couples may have a reservoir of intimacy and belongingness on which to draw, she writes, some find their interdependency in late life to be inequitably distributed and a source of conflict. The concept of equity as a criterion for happy marriages is echoed by Troll, Miller, and Atchley (1979). They state that one key finding about happy marriages is that they tend to be characterized by a much greater equality between the partners than is true of unhappy ones.

The issue of equity within the dependency relationship may be a key factor in understanding why elder abuse takes place. Kruse (1986), in a study of 60 families who were caring for chronically or terminally ill family members, suggests that aggressive behavior is a result of "psychological density." He found that both the patient and the caregiver were dependent on each other to a high degree with no outlet for their feelings, needs, or frustrations. Moreover, the longer the chronic illness lasted, the greater the danger that they would become isolated, because of their own disengagement as well as that of the social surroundings.

Whereas a change in the dependency relationship of a married couple as a result of situational factors, particularly a decline in the health of one of the partners, seems to be a likely explanation for spouse abuse, the dynamics within the family leading to parent abuse appear to be somewhat different. The four risk factors still play a role—intra-individual dynamics, dependency, stressful life events, and social isolation. The adult child in these situations, however, is often a very dependent individual who has had difficulty coping with life. Although the parent may be dependent on the child for assistance in some activities of daily living, for companionship and transportation, the adult child is often dependent on the parent for basic survival—a home and food.

Several paradigms have been postulated for explaining conflict in the relationship between parent and adult child. Cicirelli (1986) constructs a model based on attachment theory to explain adult children's neglect of their aged parents. According to the model, attachment behaviors to parents are a function of the child's prior sense of filial obligation. Children with weak attachment bonds may ignore or neglect increasingly dependent parents. Neglect also may result if the children perceive their parent's traits as undesirable or if they sense that the parents played a part in fostering a rivalrous relationship between them and their siblings. George (1986) analyzes the role of the social norms of reciprocity and solidarity in creating the stress associated with family caregiving. Under ordinary circumstances, she writes, these competing norms can be balanced, but providing care to a chronically ill older adult can lead to long-term inequality and personal distress. Neither of these models, however, adequately addresses the issue of dependent adult children, who make up a significant proportion of the abusers in this sample. The dynamics within the family setting are necessarily different when dealing with an adult child who because of mental, cognitive or alcohol problems still depends on an aged parent for physical and emotional support. While it is true that the older person under these conditions may rely on his or her child for assistance in certain tasks, in actuality the parent still has control over primary aspects of the household, especially the finances.

In the preceding analysis, the differences between spouse abuse and parent abuse have become more distinct. Elders mistreated by spouses were more often victims of physical abuse. They tended to be in poorer emotional health and to be more dependent on their abusers for companionship, financial resources and management and maintenance of property. The spousal perpetrators were more likely to have had both recent and long-term medical complaints and to have experienced a recent decline in physical health. Acts of psychological abuse and neglect committed by adult children tended to be more severe. These adult children were more likely to have money problems, to be financially dependent on their elderly parents, and to have a history of mental illness and alcoholism. Material exploitation was more common in this group than in the spouse abuse sample.

These findings confirm what might logically be assumed: that abuse or neglect perpetrated by spouses is different from that committed by adult children. Certainly, the relationships between spouses and between adult children and their parents are not identical in the shared sense of responsibility or of mutual obligation. In carrying out this particular comparison, we have become keenly aware of the need to move from general descriptive studies of elder abuse and neglect cases to more focused investigations. The results of the in-depth analysis of physical abuse cases in the next chapter is further evidence of the value of a more selective approach to studying family abuse of the elderly.

5

Understanding the Causes of Physical Elder Abuse

A special study of a sample of physically abused elders was conducted as part of the evaluation of the three Model Projects. In order to improve on previous research efforts in this area, the study had several important features. First, it focused only on one type of maltreatment: physical abuse. The sample therefore contained only elders who had experienced one or more acts of physical abuse, defined as the infliction of physical pain or injury. This act could range from throwing an object at the other person to assaulting him or her with a knife or a gun.

Second, the study did not rely, as most others have, on professional accounts of maltreatment, but instead involved direct interviews with clients. Thus, in at least in one component of the Model Projects evaluation, we were able to conduct direct interviews with victims. For this reason, the findings presented in this chapter can be used as a check on the data from case reports already analyzed. Third, and most important, the study included a matched control group of nonabused elderly. The use of a control group makes it possible to isolate factors that are associated with elder abuse, by contrasting the characteristics of the abused group with persons who are not maltreated.

An attempt was made to interview all of the physical abuse cases being

Material in this chapter appeared in slightly altered form in Pillemer 1986.

seen at the three Model Project sites during a two-month period. In some cases, this was impossible due to the unwillingness or incapacity of the clients; roughly two-thirds of the active cases were actually interviewed at each site. A control group individually matched on sex and living arrangement was selected from the nonabuse caseload of the Massachusetts project, a large, multiservice agency that served the elderly.

Case managers at this agency selected as control cases their most recent client who met the specifications provided them by the researchers; they were thus prevented from selecting particularly desirable or "interesting" cases. The case managers were asked to exclude any case in which they knew physical abuse had occurred. In spite of this restriction, three interviewees reported at least one violent incident, and were therefore excluded from the control group and replaced.

One additional aspect of the design needs mention here. In the interview with the abuse victims, many of the questions dealt with the relationship with the abuser. In the control interviews, these questions were asked about a member of the household who occupied the same relationship to the control elder. Thus, if the abuser in one case was an oldest child, the control elder's oldest child became the subject of questions.

The final sample consisted of 42 physically abused elders and 42 controls. In both groups, 39 respondents were women and three men. Both groups were predominantly white: 98 percent in the abuse group, and 95 percent of the controls. Incomes tended to be low, with 77 percent of the abuse group and 89 percent of the controls receiving less than $6,000 a year. The abused elders tended to be younger (mean age 70) than the controls (mean age 75). This is due to the inclusion of three persons aged 56, 57, and 59 in the abuse group. These three individuals were severely disabled, and for this reason Model Project staff suspended the age guidelines. Of the abusers and comparison relatives, 14 (33 percent) were husbands, 14 (33 percent) sons, 10 (24 percent) daughters, 2 (5 percent) daughters-in-law, and 2 (5 percent) brothers.

All interviews were conducted in person by the same interviewer, and lasted approximately 60 to 90 minutes. Quantitative measures were employed to explore a variety of areas: physical health, functional dependency, social support, and external stress, among others. Answers to open-ended questions were written down, and seven tape-recorded interviews (four with abuse victims and three with abusers) were conducted to obtain more detailed accounts of the maltreatment. All these qualitative data were transcribed and analyzed. The discussion in this chapter will focus primarily on the quantitative findings, although qualitative material will occasionally be used for illustrative purposes. The qualitative findings have been presented in more detail elsewhere (Pillemer 1987).

In the remainder of this chapter, we present findings related to the five risk factors identified above. In each area, a number of items were employed to operationalize the particular risk factor in question. Here, we have limited the presentation to the most important measures. The findings on the whole are relatively straightforward: a surprisingly clear and consistent picture of the abuse situation emerged.

RISK FACTOR DATA

Intra-individual dynamics

The first hypothesis to be examined is that which attributes abusive behavior to the psychological or emotional problems of the abuser. It was expected that the abusive relatives would exhibit such problems to a greater degree than the comparison relatives. The elderly respondents were asked two items related to the possible psychological impairment of their relatives. First, each respondent was asked "Does [relative] have any mental or emotional problems?" The abused elders were much more likely to report psychological or emotional problems on the part of the abuser than were nonabused elders. In fact, 79 percent of the victims reported that the relative had mental or emotional problems to some degree, compared to only 24 percent of the controls. A more objective indicator of psycho-emotional illness is psychiatric hospitalization. The relatives of the abused elderly were considerably more likely to have been placed in a psychiatric hospital than the controls (36 percent to 7 percent).

The study also examined alcohol abuse by the relatives. It was determined at the outset of the project that questions relating to this issue would not be asked directly of the respondents, due to the sensitivity of this topic, and the probability that the elders would fail to report such behavior. Instead, the caseworker involved with the victims and the controls were asked about the relatives' abuse of alcohol. This seemed a reasonable approach, as the caseworkers were very familiar with the respondents and their families. These workers were asked: "To the best of your knowledge, is [relative] an alcoholic? The abusers were significantly more likely to be identified as alcoholics (45 percent to 7 percent).

The qualitative component of the interviews also indicates that the victims frequently attributed the abuse they had suffered to pathological traits in the abuser. Many of the interviewees directly linked the maltreatment to psychosis, alcoholism, or other psychological problems. For example, in five cases, elderly women were assaulted by husbands who suffered from some form of dementia, whom they described as "out of control." Similarly, some parents reported that the abuser had suffered a "breakdown" of some kind, and began at that time to become violent. In fact, in over half of the cases, the victims cited character traits of the abuser as the primary cause of abuse. Some respondents blamed the maltreatment on substance abuse. As one mother put it: "I miss my son. But when he's on drugs, he's impossible." Sometimes they blamed themselves for the abusers' character flaws: "I raised him wrong," another mother reported. In other cases, the responsibility was placed on an "act of God." One woman reported that her son became abusive after a serious fall that caused brain damage, while others cited a stroke or Alzheimer's disease. In general, when asked "Why does he/she act this way toward you?" respondents were most likely to blame some flaw in the abuser's personality.

The question arises: Where do these findings point in our attempt to identify risk factors for elder abuse? Although the results presented here require further support and elaboration, the data argue for a consideration of individual psychopathology as a primary risk factor in elder abuse. The striking differences between the two groups on the measures described above, coupled with the victims' own perceptions, suggest that elder abusers may be especially troubled individuals. Here, we hazard one possible explanation as to why elder abusers would differ from perpetrators of other forms of family violence, who have not consistently been found to be more mentally or emotionally impaired than the general population.

Specifically, a major difference exists in the degree of normative prohibition against various types of family violence. Straus, Gelles, and Steinmetz (1980) found a great deal of popular approval for punishing children, and even a surprisingly high approval rate for spousal violence. However, it can be convincingly argued that it is a much more deviant act to strike an elderly person, and in particular a father or mother. There is no "normal" pattern for being violent towards one's elderly relatives; it is therefore a stronger normative violation than either child or spouse abuse. One might thus expect a greater degree of psychopathology on the part of elder abusers, as they engage in a more deviant behavior than others.

Such an assertion will, of course, need to be borne out by further research. The results reported here, however tentative, clearly argue for additional exploration of the role of the abuser's mental and emotional problems in maltreatment of the elderly. This focus need not have the overtone of labeling the perpetrators as "villains." It may simply mean, for example, that caregiving responsibility has fallen into the wrong hands. It is hoped that future studies will further illuminate this area.

Intergenerational transmission of violent behavior

Somewhat surprisingly, the data do not show an association between physical punishment as a child and becoming an elder abuser in later life. In those cases in which the abuser was the child of the victim, respondents were first asked an open-ended question: "How did you usually tend to punish [child] when he/she was a child and teenager?" Responses to this question were coded as either "physical punishment mentioned" or "physical punishment not mentioned." Only one interviewee in each group spontaneously mentioned using physical punishment. Instead, the typical responses were: "I didn't have to punish," and "I never hit him." Following this question, respondents were asked how frequently they had used physical punishment in the year in which they used it the most. The response categories ranged from "never" to "more than 20 times." No significant differences were found on this variable between the abuse and non-abuse groups. The same item was asked in reference to the use of physical punishment by the respondent's spouse; again, no significant differences were found. Most of the respondents reported that they had never used physical punishment, or that they had used it only once in that year.

While the data reported here are limited, they do not generally support the hypothesis that children who abuse elderly parents were themselves victims of abuse. The abuse victims reported that they rarely used physical punishment, and no difference was found between cases and controls on this issue. It is possible that this hypothesis is not a particularly promising one, and that stronger risk factors for elder abuse can be identified. Alternatively, it may be that the survey format employed in the present study is not the ideal one to obtain information regarding punishment and abuse of children. In fact, many of the respondents appeared to be uncomfortable with these questions. A future study could focus on this issue, and conduct in-depth interviews with victims regarding their relationship with the abuser in childhood. Interviews could also be conducted with abusers regarding their child and teenage years. These methods may be more effective in exploring the role of a cycle of violence in elder abuse.

Dependency

Perhaps the most important findings in the study are those on the relationship between dependency and physical abuse of the elderly. As noted, two contrasting views exist regarding the role of dependency in elder abuse. Many writers on the problem have postulated that the increasing impairment and frailty of the elderly person causes stress for the abuser, who responds with violence. We advanced an alternative hypothesis in our earlier discussion, in which abuse was attributed to a lack of power on the part of the abuser. In that case, we would expect to find perpetrators of elder abuse to be more dependent on the victims, rather than the reverse.

We will present the most important findings here; a more detailed discussion has been presented elsewhere (Pillemer 1985b). The analysis will focus on three questions. First, are abused elders, as some have asserted, more likely to be ill and to have diminished functional capabilities? Second, beyond general impairment, are abused elders specifically more dependent on the abusers than are the controls on the comparison relatives? Third, the reverse of this configuration is considered: are the abusers more dependent on their victims than are the control relatives?

The abused elderly do not, in fact, appear to be more physically impaired and in poorer health. The measure employed to test the first hypothesis is the inventory of illnesses from the Older Americans Resources and Services (OARS) instrument (Duke University Center for the Study of Aging and Human Development 1979). The abused and nonabused groups were compared on 24 conditions, ranging from arthritis and eye problems to heart disease and cancer. The respondents were asked whether they had the condition and, if so, the degree to which it interfered with their daily activities: not at all, a little, or a great deal. No significant differences ($p < .05$) were found on any of the illnesses with the exception of glaucoma; even on that condition, the difference was slight. Further, the groups did not differ significantly in whether the person was hospitalized in the past year, or in whether the respondent had experienced a decline in health status over the past five years or the past one year.

Much research has shown, however, that diagnostic condition is not as reliable an indicator of the vulnerability of the elderly as is functional impairment. That is, to what extent is the individual unable to carry out basic functions essential to daily living? Some researchers have categorized these functions as personal Activities of Daily Living ("ADLs": bathing, dressing, ambulation, etc.), and Instrumental Activities of Daily Living ("IADLs": food shopping, cooking, cleaning, etc.). Many instruments exist to assess functional status. For this study, the Index of Functional Vulnerability (IFV) was selected, which contains eleven items on mobility, orientation, and ability to perform activities of daily living (Morris, Sherwood, and Mor 1984).

The hypothesis that the dependency of the victim leads to abuse would suggest that the abused elders should be more impaired on each item of the IFV. Tests for differences between the groups, however, found that this was not the case; in fact, the reverse appeared to hold in some instances. No significant differences were found in the following variables: needing help or having great difficulty with meal preparation; being healthy enough to walk up and down stairs without help; using a walker or wheelchair at least some of the time to get around; being able to identify the correct year; the number of days on which the person went outside of his or her dwelling in the past week; being able to feed oneself; or being unable to pursue desired activities because of poor health.

These data indicate that the abused elders were not more functionally impaired than the controls in many critical ADLs. In addition, the abused group was found to be significantly less impaired than the control group in certain areas. The abused individuals were less likely to need help or have great difficulty with taking out garbage (45 percent in the abuse group to 71 percent of the controls; $p < .05$), and were more likely to report that they were healthy enough to do ordinary housework (62 percent to 38 percent; $p < .05$). The overall picture, then, is quite consistent: the abuse group is not more likely to be impaired in activities of daily living. Further, in some areas, they tend to be more independent than the controls.

Despite these findings, it could still be argued that while those in the abused group are not more impaired in general, they may be more dependent specifically on the abusers. We must ask: Do abused elders depend more on the abuser (rather than other potential helpers) than do the controls on their comparison relative? In one measure, respondents were asked whether there was someone who would care for them if they became seriously ill or disabled. Those who answered affirmatively were asked to identify the most likely helper. These responses were then coded as "Helper is abuser/comparison" or "Helper is other." The abuse group was much less likely to name the abuser as the person they would be most likely to depend on for help (26 percent to 63 percent; $p < .01$).

In another measure of the dependency of the elder on the abuser/comparison, the respondent was directly asked: "People depend on each other for many things. How much to you depend on [abuser/comparison] in each of the following areas?" Respondents were asked to answer "entirely dependent," "somewhat dependent," or "independent," in each of these areas: housing, cooking or cleaning, household repair, companionship and social activities, financial support, and transportation. No significant differences were found in five of the six areas. A difference was found in financial dependency, but the abuse group was more likely to be independent than the control group (69 percent to 48 percent; $p < .05$).

When the above measures are taken into consideration, the hypothesis that the impairment and dependency of an elderly person leads to physical abuse must be called seriously into question. None of the above data tend even slightly in that direction: either no significant differences were found, or the abuse group was less dependent than the controls. Based on the exchange perspective outlined earlier, the alternative hypothesis must be explored: that the dependency of the abuser on his or her victim is a critical predictor of abuse.

Two measures were employed to assess the extent to which the abusers or comparison relatives were dependent on the elderly respondents. The first involved a dependency index identical to that just discussed, with the questions reversed. That is, the respondent was asked: "How much does [abuser/comparison] depend on you in these areas?" The abusers were found to be significantly more dependent on the elder in four areas: housing, household repair, financial assistance, and transportation.

A second set of items was also included to examine further the imbalanced exchange between abuser and victim. The respondents were asked to imagine that they and their relative had decided to separate and establish separate residences, and that contact between them was totally broken off. They were then told: "I'm going to read you things that could be affected by a break-up like this, and for each one, I'd like you to tell me who you think would be hurt more by it: you, the abuser (or comparison relative), neither of you, or both about the same."

While the abused elders less often identified themselves as likely to be hurt the most in the areas of performing household chores, being lonely, and being able to get around, the differences were not statistically significant. However, a significant difference was found in the question of who would be hurt more financially. The abused elders viewed their relative as much more likely to be hurt financially as the result of a separation than did the control group (53 percent to 7 percent; $p < .001$). This finding is of great importance especially in conjunction with the data that showed less than 36 percent of the abusers to be financially independent of their victims. Financial dependency on the part of the abuser may be an especially important predictor of violence.

The qualitative data collected in the study support the quantitative findings. If anything, the general portrait of abusers as persons with strong dependencies on their victims is even clearer than in the above discussion. To be sure, the issue of dependency is a complex one, and is likely to be mutual rather than entirely one-sided. While the predominance of cases (over two-thirds) involved abuser dependency on the abused, some relationships were at variance with that model. Here, we provide some examples of relationships in which the abuser is heavily dependent.

> The daughter of one victim moved in with her, and never contributed in any way to her mother's support. "I support her. She has epilepsy and is on disability. She's supposed to give me $50.00 a month but she never does. She even stole a $25.00 gift certificate I won. We haven't gotten along ever. It's only nice when she's not here."

> An elderly couple had both been victims of their son's violent behavior. He was 30 years old and had lived on his own until he suffered a serious head injury with resulting brain damage. After the accident, he returned to their home. His behavior was erratic and he shouted at his parents. He taunted his father, and forced his mother off the telephone. His disability pension had been cut off, and he contributed little or no money to the household. His mother was injured trying to intervene in physical conflicts between father and son.

> The daughter of an elderly woman moved in with her following the daughter's divorce. The daughter had severe emotional problems and could not work. She struck her mother and threw a pan of scalding water on her. Her mother provided for her in almost every way. "My daughter never washes the dishes or the floor. I'd like her to go out and get a job. Her being unemployed makes it harder on our relationship, especially because she needs money. I support her entirely, financially. I'm pushed to the wall and I have to do this."

An interesting variant in this category were five cases in which wives were abused by severely disabled husbands they were caring for. For example:

> A frail woman, living in an elderly housing project, had had a stable relationship with her husband. He developed Alzheimer's disease and

needed constant supervision. "He would beat me pretty bad, choke me. He grabbed me and said 'I'll kill you.'"

These case descriptions, like the quantitative findings presented earlier, call into question the image of the elder abuser as a usually stable, well-intentioned individual who is brought to violent behavior by the excessive demands of an old person. In these examples, the abusers appear as persons with few resources who are frequently unable to meet their own basic needs. Instead, they are heavily dependent individuals: sometimes children who have been unable to separate from their parents; sometimes disabled or demented spouses. Rather than being powerful in the relationship, they are relatively powerless.

The findings reported in this section have major implications for the study of elder abuse. First, based on the data presented in this section, the hypothesis that the dependency of victim on abuser causes physical maltreatment should be seriously called into question. Instead, the hypothesis that the dependency of the relative leads to abuse was generally supported. Second, the typical physically abused elder tends to be an older woman who is supporting a dependent child or a disabled or cognitively impaired spouse. She tends to perceive the exchange relationships in which she is involved as highly imbalanced in the abuser's favor. She feels that she is giving much, and receiving little.

Further research is needed to precisely specify why being dependent on an older relative would lead to violence against that individual. From the examples given above, it is clear that financial exploitation is a factor: the abuser uses force to obtain money or goods from the victim. Certainly, the mental and emotional problems many abusers experience may make them less able to resolve differences in a non-violent way. Finally, the theory, described in chapter 2, that a sense of powerlessness in other areas can lead to the use of violence would appear to apply here. While the precise dynamics of this type of relationship remain to be determined, abuser dependency should be seen as a major possible risk factor in elder abuse.

External stress

In this analysis, it was hypothesized that families in which physical elder abuse occurs would have experienced more stress from sources external to the family than the controls. It must be noted that there are many issues in the study of stressful life events that remain to be resolved. These include how long the referent period for the reporting of events should be (e.g., six months versus one year) and whether "positive" stressors, such as taking a vacation, should be included in a life-events scale. If the research project under discussion were one in which the study of stress was the primary issue, it would be important to address such technical problems. In the present case, however, the goal was simply to explore the role of external stress in elder abuse in a preliminary way.

For this reason, a relatively uncomplicated measure of stress was developed, based closely on that employed by Straus, Gelle, and Steinmetz (1980) in their national study of family violence. This stress scale employs items such as those used by Holmes and Rahe (1967). However, it uses the household, rather than the individual, as the unit of analysis, and it consists of events that are more likely to occur at the end of the family life-cycle. Thus, respondents were asked whether any of a set of events had occurred within the past year, including a death in the household, the death of a close relative of someone in the household, and divorce or marriage of a household member. Respondents were also asked whether a household member had been ill or injured in the past year; whether someone had left or joined the household; whether someone had lost a job or retired; and whether the household had changed residence.

The results of this stress scale were inconclusive. When the abuse and control groups were compared, significant differences were found on only three items: someone was arrested, someone left the household, and someone joined the household. In each case, the abuse group was more likely to have experienced the stressful event than the control group. Unfortunately, however, the responses to these questions were confounded by the abuse situation itself. That is, in these the three significant variables, the abuser was the person who was responsible for the event. In most of the incidents involving arrest, the abuser was arrested because of violence against the elderly victim. Similarly, a number of abusers entered and left the old persons' households in the same year, because the shared living situation became so tense and violent. If these three questions were dropped, none of the stress items would have been significant.

A question was also asked about chronic financial stress, which can cause high levels of tension in households. Respondents were queried: "Sometimes financial problems can create stress. Is having enough money ever a problem for you?" No significant difference was found between the two groups. Thus, the data appear to indicate that the two groups did not differ in life stress that was unrelated to the abuser. The death or illness

of household members did not strike the abusive families more frequently, nor did divorce, unemployment, or financial strain. The qualitative data do not shed much additional light on this issue. Stress was
virtually never spontaneously mentioned by the victim as an explanation
for the abuser's behavior. When asked an open-ended question—"What
do you find stressful in your life right now"—half of the respondents cited
problems in their relationship with the abuser as the major stressor, rather
than other aspects of their lives.

Two possible conclusions can follow from this evidence. The first is
that stress has not been optimally measured here, and that alternative
indicators would achieve better results. This explanation is somewhat
persuasive: future studies should employ a more detailed measure of stress,
and carefully differentiate between stressful events that are unrelated to
the abusive situation itself, and those that result from that relationship.
It may be possible, alternatively, that the hypothesis that external stress
increases the risk of elder abuse is not correct, and that no relationship
in fact exists. This last explanation is supported to an extent by the material that has been presented in previous sections. The perpetrators have
been found to have emotional problems, to be alcohol-dependent, and to
be involved in long-term dependent relationships with the victims. The
abuse may thus be more closely related to this interplay of factors than to
the effect of stressful life events.

Social isolation

As noted in chapter 1, social support has been found to be an important
moderator of life stress, and may prevent family tensions from rising to
unmanageable levels. Further, the presence of interested outsiders can make
it more difficult to abuse an elderly relative. These individuals can intervene, or can report the abuse to law enforcement or social service agencies. Thus, it is hypothesized that physically abused elders will be more
socially isolated than the nonabused control group.

An in-depth look at social support was obtained by using the Social
Resources Rating Scale (SRRS) which is part of the OARS instrument.
This scale measures the quality and quantity of relationships with family
members and friends, as well as the availability of assistance, should older
persons require it. The SRRS can be scaled into a number of indices of
social support. Significant differences were found on two of these indices.
The first index indicates the amount of contacts the old person has, coded

as "few," "adequate," or "extensive." The abused elders were more likely to have "few" contacts with family members and friends than were the controls (36 percent to 17 percent).

The second index measures satisfaction with these contacts. The data show that the abused elders were significantly more likely to find their social relationships to be unsatisfactory (39 percent to 20 percent). Another index measures the availability of help from members of the informal support network. No significant differences were found between the victims and controls. In most cases, elders in both groups did have someone who would help them if necessary.

The abused elders, then, did appear to be more isolated than non-abused elders. They tended to have fewer overall contacts and to feel more negatively about their social situations. They were not, however, less likely to have someone to help them if they required it. It may be that the critical variable is the amount of involvement of outsiders in the home; the greater this level of involvement, the less easily a relative can be abusive without incurring the cost of negative sanctions from others. Such a finding, as noted earlier, is consistent with research on other forms of family violence.

These results, of course, do not prove that elder abuse is caused by social isolation. In fact, the causal path may work in the opposite direction. That is, the abusive relative may prevent or inhibit contact with outsiders through threatening behavior or by creating conflict in order to make visitors uncomfortable. The abused elders frequently reported that the abuser had a negative impact on their contacts with others. In some cases, the abuser directly prevented interaction with friends and relatives. For example, one abusive husband forbade his wife from calling her friends. Similarly, four female respondents reported that their adult children's behavior became worse when they (the mothers) were on the telephone. One victim reported: "He makes it hard for me to talk on the telephone. He mimics me while I'm talking. Sometimes I just throw the phone down." This problem is a serious one, for the telephone is frequently the most important source of contact with others for elderly people.

Social contact was limited not only because the abuser expressly forbade it, but because others found the erratic and antisocial behavior threatening. One abused mother stated: "It's hard to invite people over. I'm embarrassed. He talks out of line sometimes." Another woman quit her "Friendly Club" because her daughter-in-law would "start screaming" whenever the club met in her home. In another case, the husband's bizarre behavior frightened his young grandson so badly that the child was never brought back to the house. Thus, the abuser can be an important factor in reducing the victim's contact with the outside world. A vicious circle appears to exist, in which persons who might be able to intervene in the situation are driven away, allowing the abuser's behavior to worsen; this, in turn, leads to further isolation.

SUMMARY

In this study, forty-two physically abused elderly persons were matched with a non-abused control group to identify factors associated with this type of maltreatment. Five potential causes of abuse were examined: intra-individual dynamics, intergenerational transmission of violence, dependency, external stress, and social isolation. It will be useful here to recapitulate the major findings.

1. *Intra-individual dynamics.* The abusers were much more likely than the comparisons to be identified as having mental and emotional problems, and as abusing alcohol. They were also more likely to have been hospitalized for psychiatric reasons.

2. *Intergenerational transmission.* Findings in this area were not significant. Abused elders did not report more physical punishment of children, nor did they indicate that the perpetrator had been a victim of child abuse.

3. *Dependency.* Abused elders were not found to be more ill or functionally disabled than the control group; in fact, they were less impaired in a number of areas. The abuse group was not more dependent on their kin than the comparisons for assistance with activities of daily living. However, the abusers were more likely to be dependent on their elderly victims than were the control relatives.

4. *External stress.* These findings were somewhat ambiguous. While abusive families were more likely to experience three stressors (someone moving in, someone leaving the household, and someone getting arrested) these were usually actions of the perpetrator directly related to the abuse situation. The other, truly external events did not significantly differ between the two groups.

5. *Social isolation.* The abuse group scored more poorly on two social resources scales. They had fewer overall contacts and were less satisfied with those they did have.

Certainly, these findings need to be replicated by future researchers. Based on the results presented here, however, it is possible to speculate on a configuration of factors that could place older persons at risk of abuse. In this simple model, the abuser's mental and emotional difficulties, including alcohol abuse, lead in some cases directly to violence. They also cause the abuser to be dependent on the victim, which, following the exchange paradigm, can also lead to physical abuse. Social isolation is in a sort of "negative feedback loop" with dependency: the isolation of the elder keeps others from intervening to change the abuse situation, but it is also a consequence of the abuser's behavior.

It is very encouraging to note that the pattern of relationships reported in this chapter confirm the findings from the study of caseworker's reports in chapters 3, 4, and 5. Using two very different methods of collecting data, the studies have produced results that are remarkably similar. Both approaches have disclosed the poor psychological state of the perpetrators and their dependency on the victim as recurring themes in cases of physical abuse, along with the relatively independent functional status of the victims. These findings are all the more noteworthy since they run counter to the popular view of elder abuse which portrays victims as very dependent individuals and perpetrators as overburdened caregivers. The role of two other risk factors, social isolation and stress, in the two sets of analyses is also revealing. According to both studies, these families do tend to have fewer social contacts than those without violence. They may also be subjected to more stressful life events, although the data are less clear.

With this chapter, we end our detailed analysis of the nature and dynamics of elder abuse and neglect cases. Profiles of different types of maltreatment have been created, with a special focus on physical abuse. In addition to a general picture of the overall sample, we examined elder abuse committed by spouses and children and found significant differences between the two groups. Finally, by employing a case-comparison design, the study was able to pinpoint risk factors for maltreatment.

The Model Projects evaluation, however, was not restricted to an analysis of case level data. Its other major goal was to shed light on the process of intervention with families in which elder abuse and neglect occur. The next chapter describes the treatment strategies used by the Model Projects and their effectiveness in case resolution.

6

Elder Abuse Intervention: What Works?

FROM the analysis of physical, psychological and material abuse and neglect, our attention now turns to the service system. What resources were used by the projects? How successful were the projects in reducing abuse and neglect? What factors contributed to the resolution of the cases? Of course, it is impossible to answer these questions definitively. For the first time, however, we have data with which to explore these issues.

Working closely with the Worcester Model Project staff, we designed a second assessment form (case-reassessment) to measure the status of the abuse situation six months after intake and at six month intervals thereafter and/or at case closing. Since it often took several weeks to gather the baseline information, it became impractical for the staff to complete more than one reassessment. Consequently, the form was used at the close of the case, or at the end of the project period if the case was still active. The average number of months between the initial and outcome assessment was seven for the Worcester case load; eleven for Syracuse; and nine for Rhode Island.

As a companion to the case assessment, the reassessment form repeated the questions on the manifestations of abuse, dependency ratings, mental and emotional status, stress and social isolation, and added items on agency and case outcome. Data were completed on 309 cases (Worcester, 57; Syracuse, 127; and Rhode Island, 125). There were nineteen cases that could not be reassessed because they were resolved at the time of intake; they involved clients and/or families who refused to see the staff after the initial encounter; or the clients moved to unknown locations or out of state.

To analyze the data gathered at two points in time for each case, the Wilcoxin Matched-Pairs Signed Ranks test was selected. With this procedure, significant change is based both on the direction and the magnitude of the difference between the pairs. Because we were interested in the effectiveness of each project, the client data were analyzed individually for each site.

INTERVENTION

Referral patterns and mandatory reporting

Almost one-half of the Worcester cases were referred from private agencies. Other sources, such as self-report, family members, hospitals and public agencies, each accounted for about one-eighth of the case load. Only one case was referred by a private physician, and none by members of the legal profession. One in two of the Syracuse cases came from public agencies; and one in eight from members of the victims' families, with very few referrals from other sources. Two cases were referred by lawyers, and none by private physicians. The largest proportion of cases was reported to the Rhode Island Project (almost one out of four) by public agencies and slightly less than one out of five from private agencies. Self-report cases comprised about one out of six in the case load. Two situations were reported by private physicians, and three by lawyers (table 6.1).

Not unexpectedly, the case reporting patterns above show some variation, with the Worcester project receiving the largest proportion of reports from private agencies, and Syracuse from public agencies, a reflection of the different response systems for dealing with protective service cases associated with each of these localities. In Massachusetts, the responsibility for delivering social services to the elderly was transferred from the Department of Public Welfare to the Executive Office of Elder Affairs and its network of 27 home care corporations, one of which was Elder Home Care Services of Worcester Area (EHC). As a "quasi-public" agency, EHC was the local referral organization. On the other hand, in New York, the authorized agency to receive reports was the Adult Protective Ser-

TABLE 6.1: Source of case referral to the model projects

	Worcester (n = 59)		Syracuse (n = 135)		Rhode Island (n = 134)	
	#	%	#	%	#	%
Private agency	28	48	21	16	24	8
Public agency	7	12	66	49	37	28
Hospital or clinic	7	12	8	6	9	7
Client (self-report)	7	12	3	2	21	16
Member of client's family	7	12	16	12	24	18
Client's friend or neighbor	4	7	8	6	12	9
Police	—	—	2	2	4	3
Private physician	1	2	—	—	2	2
Lawyer or paralegal	—	—	2	2	3	2
Co-worker	3	5	—	—	1	1
Other	4	7	20	15	7	5

NOTE: Columns add to more than 100 percent because of multiple responses.

vices (APS) unit within the Department of Social Services. During the course of the demonstration, the local APS office transferred their elder abuse and neglect cases to the Syracuse Project which accounts for many of the public agency referrals. Additionally, the Syracuse Project received referrals from the county health department, a major health agency in that community. Public agency referrals made up the largest proportion of Rhode Island cases, no doubt because of the close relationship between the Rhode Island Department of Elderly Affairs and other state agencies, such as the Department of Social and Rehabilitative Services and the Department of Mental Health. A more detailed description of the implementation and coordination processes of the Model Projects will be presented in part 3.

This comparison of referral sources provides an opportunity to examine the impact of mandatory reporting since, of the three sites, only Rhode Island was operating under a mandatory reporting law during the course of the demonstration. Although the Worcester and Syracuse projects were not mandated to receive reports by law, they were recognized as the lead agencies in their respective communities to handle elder abuse and neglect cases.[1] If the referral patterns are examined closely, no significant

1. Local agencies were surveyed two years apart in each of the project sites to determine the impact of the Model Projects in the area. To learn more about the community response system

increase in the number of cases referred by professionals (doctors, law-yers, police) because of the mandatory reporting legislation is noted. The Worcester project received 2 percent of their referrals from this group; Syracuse, 3 percent; and Rhode Island, 7 percent, a larger percentage than either of the two other projects, but still only a small number of reports. A greater proportion of Rhode Island referrals did come from victims and family members than occurred in Worcester of Syracuse. However, nei-ther victims nor family members are generally included as mandated re-porters. We suggest that the increase in reporting by these groups is a result of the media attention given to the passage of the law, the publicity about "where to turn" for help, and the public education campaign of the Rhode Island project, particularly among the elders in the state.

In fact, if we look at the number of cases and the proportion of the population base they represented in the respective localities, mandatory reporting made little, if any, impact. At the end of the two-year data collection period, the Worcester project had handled 59 cases in an area with a population of 52,000 persons 60 years and older; the Syracuse project, 135 cases in their service area of 72,000 persons 60 years and over; and the Rhode Island project, 134 cases in a state with 177,000 persons 60 years and older. These numbers refer to substantiated cases. We do know that the Rhode Island program responded to over 400 refer-rals, many more than the other two projects.[2]

Service delivery

In answer to a question about the services utilized by the victims just prior to the agency's intervention, the Worcester staff cited health services in almost two out of three cases and informal support in one out of two. Relatively few abused or neglected elders were involved with some of the traditional aging network programs, such as meals-on-wheels, senior cen-

---

for elder abuse and neglect cases in the three sites, community agencies were asked to name, "the agency(ies) you would think of turning to if you had a case of elder abuse or neglect." The Model Projects were named by a preponderance of the respondents: 68 percent of the Worcester area agencies; 87 percent, Syracuse; and 74 percent, Rhode Island. When the question was re-worded to "the agency you turned to when you had a case of elder abuse or neglect," 83 percent of the Worcester area agencies named the Model Project; 69 percent, Syracuse; and 86 percent, Rhode Island. Source: Rosalie S. Wolf, Michael A. Godkin, and Karl A. Pillemer. "Elder Abuse and Neglect," pp. 337–342.

2. Another piece of evidence regarding the impact of mandatory reporting was given in chap-ter 3. We found very little variation in the victims and perpetrator characteristics. In fact, ex-cept for the age of the perpetrator, which was younger than the average for the Worcester and Syracuse groups, the samples were statistically alike on the demographic and health variables.

ters, legal services or volunteers. Three-quarters of the Syracuse case load received health services, but much fewer, informal support services or homemakers. Again, senior centers, legal services, or outreach programs were rarely mentioned. More than four out of five Rhode Island cases were using health services; about one out of two, informal supports; and one out of five, homemakers. A small number had been receiving meals on wheels, legal services, volunteers, and attending senior centers.

To determine the resources utilized by the Model Projects in the treatment of the cases, we asked the case workers to specify the various agencies to which they had made referrals for each of their cases in the following categories: medical, mental health, social services, volunteers, police, legal, and other. For most Worcester cases, there was one referral per category, although on behalf of one client, the staff made four "medical" contacts (physician, dental clinic, eye specialist, and home health agency.) The rank order of types of agency referrals were medical, mental health, social service, legal, police and volunteer. Housing, foster care, day care, and meals-on-wheels were included in the "other" services category and were utilized by a small minority of cases. The greater proportion of referrals in the Syracuse case load was to social service, then medical, mental health, volunteer groups, police and legal services. Under the "other" category, the Syracuse Project listed their own aide program and parish priests/outreach workers. The Rhode Island project staff made most referrals to social service agencies, followed by medical care, mental health services, police, legal services and volunteer groups. Listed under "other" were housing, employment and priests.

A separate group of questions was included on legal strategies, the first of which asked whether the caseworker thought any legal action was appropriate. For about one-third of the Worcester and Rhode Island cases, the answer was "yes"; and for not quite half, "not sure." Syracuse case workers believed that legal action would have been appropriate in only one-ninth of their cases. When requested to specify the type of legal action, the three project caseworkers most often stated "order of protection." "Criminal action", "involuntary commitment," and "competency rulings" were other legal strategies named, but restricted to only a few cases.

To the question of whether legal intervention had been initiated or planned, the Worcester staff replied "yes" for about one in four of their cases; Rhode Island for one in ten; and Syracuse for less than one in thirteen. As to the impact of mandatory reporting on case outcome, the Worcester staff believed that it might have helped to bring about an earlier or more effective outcome in about one out of six of their cases; Syracuse acknowledged that one in eight might have been improved. (Mandatory reporting was already in effect in Rhode Island.) There were similar variations in the responses when the staff was asked about the use of a short-term, involuntary protective removal law in bringing about a more effective outcome. The Worcester group thought it would have been beneficial in only four percent of their cases; the Syracuse staff thought that it would have helped about 18 percent; and according to the Rhode Island project, about 26 percent of their cases might have benefited.

A review of the Model Project service patterns indicates that for a sizable proportion of cases, the initial action on the part of the projects was to contact agencies providing either medical or social services. Since the Worcester Project was able to arrange (and pay) directly for the delivery of social services, the project staff most often contacted outside agencies for medical care, whereas both the Syracuse and Rhode Island Project caseworkers were likely to contact social agencies first, and then medical facilities. Generally, it appears that the victims, at the time the cases were reported, were not participating in programs sponsored by the aging network, although they were receiving health services. This finding corroborates the results of the Illinois Department on Aging study (1987:10) that found 92 percent of the clients served by their elder abuse demonstration projects were not known to have been receiving services through the aging network prior to the referral investigation.

In response to the question concerning legal intervention, there were some differences in opinion among the three project staff members as to whether legal action was appropriate, with the Worcester social workers assuming the most positive stance and actually using legal instruments in a larger proportion of their cases than the other two project personnel.

From these service data, the workings of the Model Projects become a little clearer. A useful characterization is the one that was described in a study commissioned by the Illinois Department on Aging (Crouse et al. 1981) and that, in fact, became the basis of a demonstration project carried out by the Department (IDA 1987). The Rhode Island project more closely resembles the "child abuse" model, since it includes mandatory reporting by professionals, reporting requirements, education about issues of elder abuse, and a time specification for contacting the victim. The "advocacy" model best reflects the approach of the Syracuse project, which did not develop a new program, but coordinated existing community services with the staff acting as advocates to guarantee and protect the victim's rights. In this model, the lowest level of intervention is prescribed.

Although the Worcester staff also acted as advocates for their clients in obtaining medical benefits and other services, they also used legal strategies more often than the other two projects, and thus may be described as a "legal model."

Barriers to service delivery

The last question on the case assessment form listed 12 barriers to effective service delivery, which the social workers were asked to rate in terms of the degree to which they had hindered or were likely to hinder the delivery of appropriate services to the case (not hindered, hindered a little, hindered a lot, or not applicable) (see table 6–2). In all three proj-

TABLE 6.2: Barriers to the delivery of appropriate service

	Worcester (n = 57)	Syracuse (n = 127)	Rhode Island (n = 125)
	%	%	%
Availability of services	42	***72	*23
Bureaucratic red-tape	28	*47	25
Coordination of agencies	13	***39	4
Coordination of services	16	***42	3
Lack of protective services	17	11	**68
Lack of respite care	41	**38	*48
Lack of support groups for caretakers	37	***60	37
Legal implications and interventions	48	**48	**47
Nonreimbursement for services	14	***60	0
Number of agencies involved	11	3	0
Receptivity of victim to help	67	***72	***74
Receptivity of perpetrator to help	**83	***90	***86

NOTE: Percentages are shown for the case reassessment only. Level of significance (Wilcoxin Matched-Pairs Signed-Ranks Test) comparing assessment and reassessment data on degree of hindrance to delivery of appropriate service:
$*p < .05; **p < .01; ***p < .001$.
The statistical test uses the scale, "none," "a little," "a lot," "no longer a problem" for determining significant results.

ects, the two most often cited barriers were receptivity of the perpetrator and of the victim to accept help. Least problematic to the projects was "number of the agencies involved," followed by "coordination of services" for Worcester; "lack of protective services" for Syracuse; and "non-reimbursement for services" for Rhode Island.

The reassessment form repeated the list of barriers. A comparison of the Worcester project responses at Time 1 (case assessment) and Time 2 (case reassessment) indicated a significant reduction in the degree of hindrance only for the barrier, "the receptivity of the perpetrator to accept help," whereas for Syracuse there was a significant decrease in all barriers. The Rhode Island case data revealed a sort of midway position, with significant reductions for about half of the barriers including "receptivity of the perpetrator and victim to accept help."

Since there were no criteria established at the start of the Model Projects to measure the degree to which the various barriers interfered with the progress of the case, the responses of the project staff reflected their own professional judgment. All did agree, however, that the greatest hindrance to the delivery of services to the abused and neglected cases was the reluctance or refusal of the perpetrator and victim to accept help, although by the time the cases were closely significant improvement in overcoming this barrier had been made in half the cases.

CASE OUTCOME

Manifestations of abuse and neglect

To determine the effectiveness of the intervention by the Model Projects, we first looked at the change in the number of manifestations of abuse and neglect between Time 1 and Time 2 and then at the change in the severity of the manifestations, using a rating scale of "mild," "moderate," "severe," "questionable," and "no longer a problem." With regard to physical abuse in the Worcester case load, there was a 53 percent drop in the number of manifestations. Of the 32 manifestations of abuse present at intake (bruises, welts, burns, bone fractures, etc.), 16 were no longer a problem at the close of the case. There were fewer manifestations marked "severe" and "moderately severe" and more "mild" as well as several that were "no longer a problem." This pattern was repeated for the other forms of mistreatment, which showed a 60 percent reduction in manifestations.

The results of the Syracuse analyses indicate a similar decrease in severity and number of manifestations, but at a somewhat lower rate, 32 percent for physical abuse and about 45 percent for other types of maltreatment. Among the Rhode Island cases, there were fewer "severe" and "moderately severe" and more "mild" manifestations at the time of the closing assessment, but the total reductions were fewer than either the Worcester of Syracuse Project: 30 percent for physical abuse cases, 49 percent, psychological abuse; and 25 percent, neglect.

In addition to the number and severity of the manifestations, the assessment also requested the social workers to rate the level of threat which the behavior of the perpetrator posed for the victim. At all three sites, there was a significant reduction in the number of cases in which the maltreatment was rated as "very" or "moderately" life threatening and an increase in the proportion for which it was "not threatening at all."

Status of the victim and perpetrator

Mental health of the victim. To find out whether there had been a change in the mental health status of the victims during the course of the Model Project intervention, the caseworkers rated the victim on orientation, memory and emotional state. No significant change was noted for the three caseloads on the orientation and memory items between the first (case intake) assessment and the second (case closing). For the Worcester case load, there was no difference in the emotional state of the victims at these two points in time, but both the Syracuse annd Rhode Island Project victims showed a significant improvement.

Dependency. At the time of the reassessment, the social workers were asked to note changes in the level of dependency of the victim on the perpetrator which had occurred since the initial assessment. Six areas were listed: companionship, daily needs, financial management, financial resources, maintenance of property, and transportation. A comparison of these results with those at intake showed a decrease in the proportion of "very dependent" and an increase in the proportion of "slightly dependent" and "independent." The change in dependency was significant in all five areas given above for the Syracuse and Rhode Island case loads, but only for companionship and daily needs for the Worcester group. The results were also mixed for the change in financial dependency of the perpetrator, with significant improvement noted for the Worcester and Syracuse cases, but not for the Rhode Island ones. When a comparison was made between the severity of the problems experienced by the perpetrators at Time 1 and Time 2, the Worcester and Rhode Island cases showed no significant change. On the other hand, the Syracuse data indicated a significant reduction in the severity of alcohol abuse and mental, medical, and financial problems.

We also requested the caseworkers to record whether there had been a change in the extent of stress caused by the abused elder on the abuser, using as a rating scale "a lot," "a little," or "not at all." There was no significant difference in the two ratings for the Worcester cases but both the Syracuse and Rhode Island Projects showed a significant reduction.

In summary, it must be kept in mind that this aspect of the study was designed to document change, if any, in the abuse and neglect situations during the period of the Model Project intervention, based on the case workers' assessments. We investigated several aspects: the manifestations and severity of the abusive and neglectful acts; the dependency status of the abused and abuser; and the quality of their relationship. Although the changes in severity of the maltreatment were not submitted to statistical tests, there was considerable improvement in the number and degree of severity of the manifestations found in the Worcester case load during the course of the intervention, and a drop in the level of threat that the actions of the perpetrator posed to the life of the victim. There appeared to be some success in reducing the dependency of the abused on the abuse regarding companionship and daily needs, probably through the use of homemakers. The cognitive status and emotional health of the victims did not change nor was there any modification in the degree of stress which the victims caused the perpetrators. However, the quality of the relationship between victim and perpetrator did improve, and the financial dependency of the perpetrator on the victim did lessen.

The findings from both the Syracuse and Rhode Island assessments and reassessments show a significant change in several areas: manifestations of abuse and neglect, level of threat, and dependency of the victim. Although the cognitive status of the victims remained unchanged, there was an improvement in their emotional state. Stress on the perpetrator was reduced, and the quality of the relationship between the two parties improved. The Syracuse staff also noted a positive change in the severity of the problems facing the perpetrator and a reduction in his or her dependency on the victim for financial resources; the Rhode Island staff did not record such gains.

In reviewing these achievements, it appears that the Worcester staff, at least in their own eyes, were less successful in changing the abuse situation than either Syracuse or Rhode Island. Although all three groups of personnel noted a reduction in the manifestations of abuse and neglect, and in the dependence of the victim on the perpetrator and vice versa, the Worcester caseload showed no significant change in the level of stress caused by the victims or improvement in their emotional state or in problems facing the perpetrator, areas in which both the Syracuse and Rhode Island cases showed significant gains.

Case resolution

Besides measuring the change in individual characteristics, the evaluation also analyzed the success of the projects in resolving the cases and the factors that contributed to the resolution. "Resolution" was defined as the discontinuation or alleviation of the mistreatment. The first part of our discussion provides descriptive data by site on case resolution and the degree to which it was affected by certain events. In the second part, factors describing the characteristics of the victim, perpetrator, abuse and neglect situation, and intervention strategies are analyzed to determine their relationship to successful case resolution.

One of the questions on the reassessment form asked the caseworker to note the extent to which the case had been resolved: "completely," "a lot," "a little," or "not at all." About one-third of the Worcester and Syracuse cases were resolved and a somewhat larger proportion of the Rhode Island group. Little or "no" success was found in about one-third of the Worcester and one-fourth of the Syracuse and Rhode Island cases (table 6.3). Another question referred to the status of the victim at the time of reassessment. The responses revealed that 15 of the 127 Syracuse victims

TABLE 6.3: Extent to which cases of elder abuse were resolved

	Worcester (n = 51)		Syracuse (n = 109)		Rhode Island (n = 106)	
	#	%	#	%	#	%
Not at all	7	14	5	5	18	17
A little	11	22	20	18	10	9
A lot	14	28	49	45	34	32
Completely	19	37	35	32	44	42

had died; 8 of the 125 Rhode Island victims; and none of the Worcester elders. Approximately one-fourth of the Syracuse group were admitted to nursing or rest homes; about twice the proportion of the Worcester and Rhode Island cases. Less than one-tenth of the sample from each site was hospitalized. New housing arrangements were made for one-tenth or less of the victims in each case load. The data for the perpetrators showed that 6 of the 57 Worcester perpetrators had died and one had been admitted to a nursing home. In the Syracuse case load, 11 of the 127 had died or left the scene, and one had been placed in a nursing home. The Rhode Island records indicated that 17 of the 125 had died or were absent and three were in nursing homes. Thus, at the end of the two-year-study period, the living arrangements for almost one half of the cases had not changed (table 6.4).

We then asked the project staff to record the extent to which various interventions had contributed to the resolution of the case, grading them as "very negative," "somewhat negative," "no effect," "somewhat positive," and "very positive." So that the results could be compared across

TABLE 6.4: Status of victim and perpetrator at time of case reassessment

	Worcester n = 57		Syracuse n = 127		Rhode Island n = 125	
	#	%	#	%	#	%
Victim died	—	—	15	12	8	7
Victim in nursing home or rest home	7	12	29	23	16	13
Victim in hospital	5	9	7	6	4	3
Victim in new housing arrangement	5	9	9	7	13	11
Perpetrator died or is absent	6	11	11	9	17	14
Perpetrator is in nursing home	1	2	1	1	3	2
Housing arrangement of victim and perpetrator unchanged	33	58	72	57	62	50

NOTE: Columns add to more than 100 percent because of multiple responses (victims and perpetrators).

the sites, a rating scale was designed ranging from minus 2 (very negative) to plus 2 (very positive). According to table 6.5, which gives the group means for the eight intervention strategies, the most effective intervention for the Worcester project was "changes in social or living situation of the victim" and the least effective was activities related to the perpetrator. The order of responses for the Syracuse project was very similar to those of Worcester except for "changes in the circumstances of the victim" which the Syracuse staff reported as one of the least effective in resolving the case, but which the Worcester staff found one of the most instrumental in bringing about case resolution. The order of ratings for the Rhode Island case load was also similar to the other two projects, although "specific interventions" was even more highly rated than "changes in the social or living situation of the victim."

When the results from the three sites were compared using a scale reduced to three categories ("very and somewhat negative," "no effect,"

TABLE 6.5: Effectiveness of interventions on resolution of the abuse and neglect cases

	Worcester (n = 57)	Syracuse (n = 127)	Rhode Island (n = 125)
Changes in social or living situation of the victim*	+1.8	+1.5	+1.3
Removal of barriers	+1.5	+1.4	+1.2
Specific interventions	+1.5	+1.1	+1.4
Changes in unhealthy interdependency of victim and perpetrator	+1.4	+1.1	+1.1
Reduction in stress caused by abuse*	+1.3	+1.2	+0.8
Reduction in life problems of the perpetrator	+1.0	+0.9	+0.6
Changes in the circumstances of the perpetrator that precipitated the abuse**	+1.0	+0.7	+0.5
Changes in the circumstances of the victim that precipitated the abuse***	+1.6	+0.8	+0.7

NOTE: Rating scale: -2 = very negative; -1 = somewhat negative; 0 = no effect; $+1$ = somewhat positive; $+2$ = very positive

Chi-square level of significance based on the proportion of cases in three categories (very and somewhat negative; no effect: and somewhat and very positive):

*$p < .05$; **$p < .01$; ***$p < .001$.

and "somewhat and very positive"), there were significant differences among the three projects for four of the eight strategies: "changes in the social or living situation of the victim," "reduction in stress caused by the abuse and neglect," "changes in the circumstances of the perpetrator," and "changes in the circumstances of the victim." In each of these instances, the Worcester case workers assessed these strategies more positively than their Syracuse or Rhode Island counterparts.

Factors contributing to case resolution

For this segment of the study, the responses to the question on case resolution were decreased from four categories to two: unresolved ("not at all" and "a little") and resolved ("a lot" and "completely"). Also, this analysis was based on the total sample rather than the individual site case loads since the objective was to identify characteristics that might contribute to successful case resolution rather than to look for differences in outcome among the projects. The chi-square test was used to determine significant differences at the $p \leq .05$ level for all the variables described in chapter 3.

There was no relationship between case resolution and victim factors such as age, marital status, sex, income, use of supportive devices, number of medications, memory, self-esteem, sources of stress, and number of social contacts. Significant differences were found for temporal orientation; dependency needs related to financial resources, and transportation; and problems in personal care, general shopping and household management. In all these instances, the individual for whom the case was resolved tended to be more dependent and impaired than the victim whose case was unresolved.

None of the perpetrator variables were related to case resolution: age, sex, history of alcohol abuse, history of mental illness, unrealistic expectations of the abused, dependency in financial resources, availability of family members for support, and someone to call in a crisis. Of the situational variables tested (household composition, type of maltreatment, relationship of perpetrator to victim, perpetrator lives with victim, quality of the relationship, household income, and level of threat of the abuse and neglect), only one was significantly related to case resolution: type of maltreatment. The resolved cases were more likely to involve neglect whereas the unresolved cases were were more apt to be physical abuse.

We found many significant relationships, however, between case resolution and barriers. Expectedly, the Model Project staff encountered fewer barriers to intervention with the resolved case. The greatest differences were found in the effect of "receptivity of the victim and perpetrator to accept help." In two-thirds of the unresolved cases, receptivity of the victim hindered the intervention at least "a little," compared to one-fourth of the resolved cases. Even more striking was the finding that the abuser's lack of receptivity was a problem in four-fifths of the unresolved cases compared to about one-third of the resolved cases.

In summary, the results of the case reassessment indicate almost one third of the cases seen by the Model Projects were resolved completely, with some progress toward resolution noted for almost another third. While the underlying principle of practice for all the Model Projects was to try to keep the family unit intact, changes in the living situation were made in almost half the cases, either through departure of the perpetrator or placement of the victim in a nursing home, hospital, or new living quarters.

We utilized two approaches to determine what conditions aided in case resolution. First, the case workers were given a list of intervention strategies and asked to record to what degree they had contributed to the resolution of the case. For the three projects, "changes in social or living situation" was rated as the most effective and "changes in the circumstances of the perpetrator" as the least successful strategy. Generally, the Worcester staff tended to rate all interventions as more effective than either of the two Project staff, which is rather surprising since the Worcester Project had the largest proportion of cases in the categories of "not resolved at all" or "resolved a little."

The second approach to the question was to identify the victim, perpetrator, and situational characteristics related to case resolution using a pooled sample from the three sites. Very few significant results emerged. Case resolution was more likely to occur when the victims were dependent and neglected than when they were more independent and physically abused.

Before drawing any conclusions from these findings about successful practice or project design, we need to know more about the way the Model Projects functioned, the role of the staff, and the relationship to other community agencies. With information drawn from individual and organizational analyses, we will be in a better position to make recommendations about treatment and prevention programs. In part 3, we examine the operation of the Model Projects.

PART THREE
Organizational Analysis

Introduction

THE expansion of services to abused and neglected elders in the past decade has been extensive. In the absence of a comprehensive national policy regarding maltreatment of the elderly, states and local communities have designed their own programs to help abused elderly persons and their families. A wide variety of services has been initiated, ranging from elder protective services, to family counseling, to legal intervention. Some of the intervention strategies—such as protective services for the elderly, backed up by mandatory reporting statutes—are highly controversial (see Faulkner 1982; Crystal 1986). Debate also exists over the most appropriate direct services to elder abuse victims. Are services to caregivers the most important (Quinn and Tomita 1986) or would greater involvement of victim advocacy services and law enforcement officials be of greater use (Breckman and Adelman 1988)?

At present, one of the greatest gaps in information about elder maltreatment is evaluation data regarding various types of interventions. Little is known in particular about the actual day-to-day activities of elder abuse workers. How do elder abuse intervention projects operate in actual practice? What implementation problems do new projects encounter? How do they establish a clientele? What types of relationships exist between elder abuse projects and other agencies? Without better answers to these questions, funds may be wasted on inappropriate services which fail to help—and may even harm—elder abuse victims and their families. In part 3, we provide new data to help answer these questions, by offering a detailed analysis of the organizational structure and day-to-day operation of the Model Projects.

There are two major reasons for providing such a description. First, it is likely that other service agencies will wish to attempt to replicate one or more aspects of the Model Projects. In order to do so, they require specific information on the way in which each program operated. Because the present study represents the first systematic evaluation of alternative models of service provision to abused and neglected elders, it is important to capture and record the major intervention strategies used by each project, and to chronicle some of their successes and failures.

Second, earlier chapters have attempted to evaluate the impact of the Model Projects, with a focus on client characteristics and treatment outcomes. It is therefore necessary to describe what the projects actually *were*, and what they *did*. As two evaluation specialists (Morris and Fitzgibbon 1978) have noted, even if an outcome analysis demonstrates that a program was successful, it is incomplete without detailed information about the program itself. Outcome data, they assert, might lead one to assume that the program "worked." They continue:

> Unless you have taken care, however, to describe the program's myriad facets, you will be unable to answer the question that logically follows your judgement of program success. That question would ask; "*What* worked?" If you cannot answer that question, you will have wasted effort measuring the outcome of an event that cannot be described and must therefore remain a mystery (10).

In part 3, we provide such a description of the Model Projects.

In this introductory chapter, the methodology of the organizational analysis is discussed, and some common features of the projects detailed. Chapters 7, 8, and 9 describe each project in detail. In each chapter, three basic issues are discussed in turn. These are:

1. *Basic features of the model.* What were the principal components of each Model Project? How did each project operate on a daily basis? What were the major activities of the staff? What were the services provided by the project?

2. *Implementation.* What was the history of each project? What unique factors in the community service environment influenced its development? What implementation problems were encountered? How were such problems overcome? What was the relationship between the Model Project and the agency in which it was located?

3. *Interagency coordination.* How did coordination with other agencies take place? How did each Model Project interact with other agencies in the areas of referrals, service utilization, and ongoing case management? What sorts of formal and informal linkages existed?

Method

A variety of data collection techniques were employed to answer the above research questions. The major component involved in-depth interviews at each of the three sites, which were tape-recorded and transcribed. The two project staff at each site were interviewed, as were other personnel in the agency that sponsored the project. The latter individuals included the agency director, directors of other agency programs, and direct service staff. In addition, persons from four or five other community agencies were interviewed regarding their perception of and contact with the Model Project.

Model project staff and the personnel from other community agencies were also administered a standard assessment tool, the Organizational Assessment Instrument (OAI) which was adapted for the present study (Van de Ven and Ferry 1980). The OAI identifies organizational characteristics that explain the effectiveness of an organization and the quality of work life. One component of the OAI was given to project staff, which asked about basic work activities and the type and quality of contact with others in the agency and in other agencies. Another form was given to persons in other agencies identified by the Model Project as the agencies with whom it had the most intensive coordinative relationships during the previous six months. Rhode Island and Worcester identified five such agencies, and Syracuse four.

There were some obvious similarities and differences in these choices. All three projects selected a home health agency and a senior or neighborhood center. Both Syracuse and Rhode Island named Adult Protective Services, which were not available in Massachusetts. Rhode Island and Worcester identified a mental health agency as an important service, while Syracuse did not. Finally, each project had one unique choice: Rhode Island named the police department; Syracuse, an information and referral hotline; and Worcester, a legal services corporation. Thus, while coordination with certain agencies appears to be important across sites, specific program factors or historical relationships may influence reliance on other particular agencies.

A final data-gathering technique was observation. A member of the evaluation team visited each site several times over the course of the demonstration, and accompanied workers on home visits to clients. Project staff meetings were observed, as well as conferences with staff from other agencies.

Common elements of the model projects

In general, the basic design elements were quite similar in all three Model Projects. The Model Projects shared similar objectives that they attempted to achieve throughout the course of the demonstration. All three projects had the primary purpose of providing casework services to abused and neglected elders (persons 60 and over) and members of their families. The goal was to intervene in cases of maltreatment, to introduce services where appropriate, to counsel victims and relatives, and to help resolve conflict between abuser and abused. In addition, the Model Projects were also to fulfill the important function of coordination among other service providers. They were to serve as a focal point for attempts by local agencies to help abused clients. Finally, all three projects had as a goal the education of community residents regarding the problems of elder abuse and neglect. Each was to organize training and information sessions on the topic.

Thus, one common element of the projects was similar goals. Another point of similarity was the target population to be served. First, the projects only handled abuse and neglect in *domestic* settings; maltreatment in institutions was beyond the scope of the project. Second, self-neglect or self-abuse were excluded; the projects were only concerned with abuse by *others*. Third, the Projects employed identical definitions of abuse and neglect (see figure 2.1).

In addition, the staffing and funding of the three projects were similar. Each project was funded to employ a half-time director and a full-time caseworker.[1] Further, a uniform system to collect data at the three sites was instituted. The staff at all three projects used identical assessment instruments and record-keeping forms, designed by the evaluation team. The sites were visited to ascertain that the forms were understood and

1. Certain differences did exist in staffing patterns, however. For example, the Syracuse project received funds from a local agency which permitted them to hire a full-time director. Along the same lines, Rhode Island was able to employ an information and referral specialist. These differences did not substantially affect the performance of the projects.

that common definitions were being adhered to. This procedure insured the collection of comparable data from the projects.

Despite these general similarities, each Model Project represented a distinct service approach to elder abuse and neglect. It is possible to identify these models as follows. The Worcester project employed what we have termed a "service brokerage" model, in which the agency had direct control over a wide array of services that could be used to help resolve a case. A major function of the project was thus to introduce and manage those services. The Syracuse project followed a "coordination" model. Although all three Model Projects filled a coordinating role to some degree, the Syracuse project made this aspect the core of its efforts. Rhode Island's approach can be considered a "mandatory reporting" model, in that it was the only project that operated under a mandatory reporting law. [2] As the unit designated to respond to abuse reports, the Rhode Island Project emerged as a distinct model.

It would be, to be sure, misleading to characterize the Model Projects as three totally distinct intervention models. In fact, all three models acted to some degree as service brokers and coordinators. To the extent, however, that each project adopted a special focus in its activities, these labels accurately distinguish the models. In the following three chapters, the special characteristics of each Model Project are detailed. After each description, a case example is provided to illustrate the features of the intervention model and the pathway of a typical client through the process. Next, implementation issues are discussed. Each chapter closes with an analysis of interagency coordination.

2. In July of the last year of the demonstration (1983), a mandatory reporting law was passed in Massachusetts. The data for the organizational analysis, however, were collected prior to this law's passage.

7

Massachusetts: A Service Brokerage Model

THE Massachusetts project was located in Elder Home Care Services of Worcester Area, Inc., a large multiservice agency that provides nonmedical home care services to persons over the age of 60. Elder Home Care Services (EHC) is a "Home Care Corporation" (HCC), a type of service provider unique to Massachusetts. To understand the nature of the Worcester project, it is necessary to briefly describe the HCC system.

The Massachusetts Executive Office of Elder Affairs maintains purchase agreements with 27 HCCs across the state. HCCs directly provide case management and information and referral services, and contract for a range of other services, including homemaker and chore services, transportation, congregate and home-delivered meals, and legal aid. Case management is a particularly important component of the HCCs. All clients who request services are initially prescreened by intake workers. If the client meets basic eligibility guidelines, he or she is referred to a case manager. Using a standard form called the Comprehensive Needs Assessment Procedure (CNAP), the case manager performs a detailed assessment of the client. Based on this evaluation, a plan of care is developed.

Applicants who are determined to be ineligible for HCC services are assisted by an information and referral specialist in finding another appropriate provider. Clients who are accepted are assigned permanent case managers who, in addition to developing the care plan, are responsible for initiation and monitoring of service delivery and periodic reassessment of client need until the case is closed due to death, institutional placement, or lack of need for services.

During the Model Projects evaluation, most HCCs did not have specially trained protective service workers. Instead, case managers handled the few cases of maltreatment that appeared in their caseloads. EHC departed from this basic model when it instituted first a crisis-intervention project, and later the elder abuse project. It thereby offered case managers an unusual opportunity to seek assistance in abuse and neglect cases, or to transfer cases entirely to a specialized intervention program.

The Model Project at EHC operated as part of a protective services unit that consisted of the elder abuse social worker, a crisis-intervention worker who handled nonabuse cases, and a director who devoted half of his time to the supervision of each of these workers. The director also took a certain number of cases as his own clients.

An important feature of the Worcester model was that for most abused clients, Model Project staff served as the HCC case manager. When an abuse case was referred from another agency, the social worker or director performed the initial assessment, developed a plan of care, and initiated services. If the abused individuals met eligibility requirements, the worker could provide them immediately with a homemaker, home-delivered meals, or other services. This is an extremely critical point: EHC abuse workers had the ability to offer a client concrete home care services in addition to counseling or legal intervention.

Although most Worcester abuse cases were eligible for state-financed home care services, some were financially ineligible for services, or were unwilling to go through the application process. In such instances, the elder abuse workers could bring in services in some other way: for example, some services were financed by federal Title III funds, and thus had no financial eligibility guidelines. Other services were financed directly from the elder abuse grant. Elder abuse workers could call on two full-time geriatric aides funded by the project, without going through the cumbersome eligibility determination process.

As will become apparent below, it was this use of services that differentiated Worcester most clearly from the other projects. The Rhode Island project had much more limited access to home care services of this type, and the Syracuse project made use only of specialized elder abuse aides. The Worcester project alone was able to directly provide a wide range of services to clients.

Homemaker services were most frequently used. They could be authorized up to four hours a day, five days a week. Thus, Worcester staff could effectively monitor an abuse or neglect situation through the homemaker, while relieving stress on the parties involved by helping them with cooking, cleaning and food shopping. Meals-on-wheels, chore services, and friendly visitors were also used by staff to perform a monitoring function.

Beyond providing services, staff in the Worcester project attempted to establish a counseling relationship with both abuser and abused. Often, the worker was involved with a client for a long period of time, and assisted him or her in taking steps to improve the situation. Further, the relationship could go beyond a standard therapist-client relationship: Worcester project staff often provided a wide range of assistance to clients. As one worker commented:

> Although it's a professional relationship with the person, it also has a quasi-personal feeling about it. I think many times, we can have the flexibility to do things, like take someone in our car if it's necessary, and just do little personal things like that. That's the kind of stuff that goes to the core of the relationship, and what I consider to be a real important feature.

It is important to point out that as a result of these features, Worcester project staff tended to have long-term relationships with their clients to a greater degree than the other sites. Since the abused individuals were likely to become clients of the *agency*, as well as the abuse unit, opportunities for monitoring and follow-up were greater. Worcester served fewer total abuse and neglect cases than the other two projects, perhaps due to a more enduring and intensive relationship with clients who were seen by the project.

In summary, the Worcester project had a number of distinct characteristics. First, it was located in a large elder service agency. As workers in that agency, project staff had considerable leeway in using a wide array of services to intervene in abuse situations. They also counseled clients and assisted them in variety of other ways. Because of the nature of this project, involvement with clients tended to be long-term. An additional aspect of the model—coordination of the activities of other agencies—is discussed in a later section.

As a way of making this somewhat abstract discussion more concrete, a specific case example will be presented here. Following this case, the typical pathway of a client through the Worcester project will be described.

Case example

Agnes was a 63-year-old woman who lived with her brother Edward, also in his sixties. Another sister referred Agnes to the Crisis Intervention worker. The sister felt that physical abuse was taking place; she reported that Agnes' glasses had been broken, and her face was bruised. She also informed the Crisis Intervention worker that the brother would talk about having to "discipline" the sister. The Crisis Intervention worker promptly referred this case to the elder abuse project, and ceased to be involved in the case.

The elder abuse team took on the case, and ascertained that physical abuse had indeed occurred. Edward complained that Agnes "drove him crazy" by following him around the apartment and leaving notes for him. During the time she was working outside of the home, he claimed, things had been fine. Her health status, however, had recently declined to the extent that she had been forced to quit her job, and was now virtually homebound. He was also angry that her only financial contribution to the household was her social security check. As a result of these strains, the brother would, according to the caseworker, "lose his ability to cope." He would then lash out violently on occasion.

The abuse unit arranged for a psychiatric evaluation of both parties. The psychiatrist reported that Edward had serious psychiatric problems. At this point, the two abuse workers decided to divide the case, with the social worker taking Agnes as her client, and the project director seeing Edward. They quickly found the brother to be openly threatening towards his sister, and the two argued violently. In fact, their repeated verbal battles had brought them to the verge of eviction from their apartment. Through interviews with the pair and contacts with other involved agencies, the abuse workers learned that the brother had been in a mental hospital for over twenty years and was discharged into his sister's care. This tenuous arrangement broke down when the sister became unemployed. Based on their assessment of the situation, the major goal of the abuse workers became the permanent separation of the two individuals.

Before that could be accomplished, the police intervened during a particularly bad fight. Edward was jailed overnight. The project director met with him and attempted to persuade him to move away from his sister. He refused, citing his reliance on his sister's social security income. During this time, the abused woman moved in with her sister. The director assisted the brother, even appearing with him in court, and helping him get a continuance, on the condition that he undergo psychiatric treatment.

The social worker continued to work with the abused woman, who was now residing with her sister. The worker arranged for a geriatric aide to be sent in three times a week. She also attempted to enroll Agnes in an adult day health program, but this was not successful, due to her agitation at the center. During this period, the sister with whom Agnes was temporarily residing became increasingly hostile and uncooperative. It became apparent that another living situation would have to be sought. The social worker continued to work with Agnes, and provided her with additional services. She arranged for more psychiatric visits, and obtained dentures for her. Agnes also received home health services, and the social worker stayed in close contact with the home health agency for coordination purposes.

The situation appeared to be reaching resolution when Agnes expressed a desire to enter a nursing home. The social worker packed her belongings and took her to a facility with an available bed. As the intake process dragged on, Agnes became increasingly upset, and demanded to be taken back to her sister's home.

Shortly thereafter, the abuse unit learned that Agnes had other relatives living in Kentucky. They were contacted, and were very concerned about the situation. They came to Worcester, and worked intensively with the Model Project staff. The relatives were granted guardianship of Agnes, and took her back with them to Kentucky where she agreed to be placed in a nursing home.

Throughout this time, the Model Project director worked with the brother. He gave Edward financial counseling and assisted him in locating new housing. Edward was able to continue living independently, without the assistance of his sister.

A number of features of the Worcester Model are illustrated by this case. First, the staff brought in services (geriatric aide, legal assistance) over which they had direct control. Second, they engaged in extensive coordination with other agencies. In fact, this case involved interaction with a wide array of service providers: a home health agency, the police, the courts, legal services, a nursing home, an adult day health center, and a dentist, as well as services provided by EHC. This demonstrates the workers' twin roles as service broker and coordinator. Finally, both staff members acted as counselors to the clients, and supported them through difficult life circumstances. Although the workers' involvement in this case was perhaps unusually intense, it gives a sense of the broad range of their activities.

Client pathway. It is possible to summarize the usual way in which clients proceeded through the Worcester project. Clients came from a wide variety of referral sources. When community agencies suspected abuse, the most likely agency in the area to contact was EHC. After the referral, Model Project staff verified the existence of abuse and neglect. If no maltreatment was found, the client might be referred into the basic HCC program.

If abuse was identified or highly suspected, the project's first step was to contact other agencies involved with client to determine the role the abuse unit should play. If, after such consultation, the Model Project staff determined that their involvement would be useful, they made a home visit. The purposes of this encounter were to verify whether abuse or neglect were actually occurring and to identify who in the client's support network could be called in for assistance on the case. The workers also attempted to gather detailed information on the history of the case and its current dynamics. Following this visit, additional consultation with other agencies usually took place.

A plan of intervention was then designed for the case. Often, this involved the introduction of services. It also frequently included long-range goals, such as separating the abuser from the abused by commitment, institutional placement, or some other means. If all parties in the situation were cooperative, then the agreed-upon services were either directly authorized (if they were HCC services) or were arranged for from another agency. If one or both clients were either uncooperative or possibly legally incompetent, various legal alternatives were sometimes pursued before services could be arranged. Project staff then followed the case until it was closed due to relocation of the client or abuser, or cessation of the abuse.

This client pathway model is of couse an oversimplification and idealization of what could often be a highly variable process. It does highlight in a general way, however, the major features of the Worcester Model: service authorization, coordination with other agencies and the informal support network, counseling, and case monitoring.

PROJECT IMPLEMENTATION

The Worcester Model Project was located in a Home Care Corporation that serves over 2,100 elderly persons in the city of Worcester and fifteen surrounding towns. In the late 1970s, the agency began to encounter crisis and emergency situations in growing numbers, and found that such cases involved complex legal, medical, and psychiatric issues. Case managers in the agency had neither the skills nor the time to handle such complicated problems. Other agencies in the Worcester area were simultaneously looking for new ways to deal with elders in crisis situations.

In response to this perceived need, the board of directors of EHC decided to improve the agency's ability to respond to crises, and in general to develop greater expertise in this area. To achieve these goals, the Crisis Intervention Program was established in 1977, with the aid of a grant from the local Area Agency on Aging. A social worker with considerable experience in working with the elderly was hired, who began to assist older persons in crisis situations. She also established linkages with other providers, including legal, medical, psychological, and health services. The crisis intervention worker intervened in cases of eviction, self-neglect, maltreatment by others, and similar problems.

By 1980, when the Administration on Aging solicited proposals for the Model projects on Elder Abuse, the Worcester Crisis Intervention Program had already established itself within the community and had gained considerable experience with elder abuse and neglect cases. It was thus perceived by persons both inside and outside the agency as a logical location for the funded project. EHC staff met with personnel from the Massachusetts Executive Office of Elders Affairs, and a joint application was decided upon.

Community agency personnel interviewed in this study were in agreement that EHC was the logical choice for the project. A Visiting Nurse Association official asserted that "Elder Home Care really has the coordinating function. They have community acceptance, and their case managers are already seeing over 2,000 cases a year. They have a broad base, a broad constituency." An EHC administrator highlighted the services offered by the agency: "Because many [abuse] cases need some of our services, it's much easier just to plug them right into what we already have, so that it's easier for the crisis unit to get in a homemaker or transfer a patient or whatever. They are right here where the services are being provided."

EHC was viewed, then, as the most appropriate agency in the region for the project. This concensus was probably responsible for the lack of "turf" issues during the project's implementation. Although such issues were not absent in the community, few problems were encountered with other service providers. Since a Crisis Intervention Program already existed, other agencies were accustomed to making referrals to EHC. When asked what difficulties other agencies might have in implementing an elder abuse project, the project director noted: "I think starting from cold they would have more difficulty than we did, because we inherited a situation where there was an understanding that the agency dealt with crisis cases, so all this really did was to expand our case ability. Essentially, it just added more staff . . . I think an agency starting from scratch would have to develop a reputation."

The project director devoted a considerable amount of time in the early months of the demonstration to agency outreach. He visited sixty to seventy different agencies and organizations, informing them about the project, and discussing elder abuse. In those meetings, he reported, "What you would be doing is kind of introducing yourself, what your training is, what your background is, what you're going to try to do, to try to inspire some confidence and hopefully generate some referrals." This process was facilitated, he added, by the receptive nature of the existing service network: "There was a good network in the community and there was a good relationship among the people who were in the network."

An important implementation problem developed in the Worcester project that was due to the specific nature of the project design. As mentioned above, EHC employs case managers, each of whom is responsible for the assessment and monitoring of a number of elderly clients. The case manager serves as the service broker for these clients, and visits each individual once every 90 days. In addition to having official responsibility for their case load, case managers frequently develop close personal attachments to their clients.

The elder abuse project staff, too, were "case managers," in that they had the same responsibilities for their abuse and neglect caseload, including assessment, monitoring, service planning, and regular visits. Thus, there was considerable overlap of responsibility between the abuse staff and case managers, which had the potential to cause conflict. In its simplest form, the issue was as follows: If a case manager reported that a client was abused or neglected, who would take charge? Did the case manager, who might have already developed rapport with the client, continue to manage the case? Or did the project staff take over, because of their specialized expertise? Due to this somewhat complicated situation, the Worcester project was forced to deal to a greater degree with intra-agency issues, while Rhode Island and Syracuse largely were not. It is therefore appropriate to focus on the challenges Worcester faced, and the solutions that were developed to meet them.

The first critical issue in intra-agency coordination at EHC was when a case manager sought to refer a case to the project. According to the intake services supervisor, the original question was "When do you bring a case to [the project]? I think there was a period at the beginning when experienced case managers were trying to handle abuse cases on their own. We really had to come down hard on them at some point and say if there is anything that shows any type of abuse, it has to go through [the project]." Thus, in theory at least, all cases of suspected abuse were expected to be referred to the elder abuse project.

The usual pattern, when abuse was suspected, was for the case manager to bring it to the attention of his or her supervisor, who then reported it to the project director. Following this action, one of the three basic methods of handling the case were employed. These were as follows:

1. The abuse unit took over the case completely. The project staff member became the case manager, and relieved the individual who referred the case of all responsibility for it.

2. The project worker could act strictly in a consulting role, advising the case manager as needed, but not assuming the management of the case in any way. This generally occurred when the existence of abuse was questionable.

3. The project worker and the case manager could "co-manage" the case. Under this arrangement, both parties retained a strong hand in the case, and planned the intervention jointly. This tended to occur when abuse or neglect was determined to exist, but when the case manager had already established a strong relationship with the client.

As these options indicate, a considerable amount of negotiation had to take place between project staff and case managers. Many of the case managers who were interviewed felt initially confused about the project's role and its impact on their duties. Some felt that their ability to manage cases as they saw fit was being circumscribed.

Because of this overlap in duties and the resulting confusion and concern, coordination within the agency became a major issue in the Worcester project, one that required extensive attention and was perceived as an important area for project improvement. The problem appears to have been due to the particular structure of EHC. Unlike the other Model Projects, EHC employs workers with responsibilities that mirrored substantially those of the project staff.

This tension was reflected in the fact that every respondent in EHC— administrators, supervisors, case managers, and project staff—noted that improving communication between the project and case managers was an important on-going agency goal. Thus the project director observed that "we may not do as good a job as we should about making everybody aware of exactly what it is we're doing." A case manager confirmed this opinion: "The major problem that I've perceived with this project is lack of communication. There wasn't nearly enough feedback from either of the two workers involved [in one case]. My own suggestion would be that the [project] be more open to sharing information with the case managers."

We have touched on these internal problems not to highlight weaknesses specific to EHC. Rather, it is extremely likely that such difficulties will occur in *any* agency with a similar structure. The other two projects were free of such problems simply because they did not have workers similar to EHC case managers. Any agency that structurally resembles EHC should prepare itself to encounter problems of intra-agency coordination.

It is to EHC's credit that these problems were openly recognized and discussed. The project staff were very open to criticism in this area, and attempted to overcome it. For example, over the course of the demonstrations, more formalized methods for referral of cases to the project were developed. At the time of the interviews, staff in-service trainings were being planned, and a number of other options to increase communication were under consideration. It is particularly important to note that all interviewees were *in general* highly satisfied with the project and felt that it had had a positive impact on the agency. Improvements in communication were seen as ways of further strengthening the project.

On a final note, individuals planning elder protective services must realize that the structure of a particular intervention program can bring strengths in some areas, and weaknesses in others. Although the Worcester project encountered some difficulties in intra-agency coordination, its relationship with *other* agencies was extremely smooth and problem-free: more so than at either of the other Model Projects, as will become apparent below.

INTERAGENCY COORDINATION

The Worcester project was ideally situated to assume a major responsibility for elder abuse cases. It was located in the central elder services agency in the region, one which had long been looked to for leadership in a variety of areas. As case managers, the Worcester project staff were able to personally authorize a wide variety of services for their clients, including homemaker, chore, transportation, and nutrition services. This combination of organizational prestige and control over resources made the project staff likely to take coordinative responsibility for a case rather than other involved agencies.

The Worcester project social worker described a typical example of case coordination which shows her central case management role:

> This was a man living with his daughter. I used the Age Center [a local elderly service and planning organization] initially to find an appropriate companion for him. Then, I called an adult day health center. I spoke with a social worker there, described the situation, and asked if she felt the person was basically appropriate, and what would need to be done to get him accepted there, and get some information from them regarding the program. Then I spoke with our visiting nurse liaison about the situation. I told her I wasn't really clear on the medical background: "I'm getting some fuzzy stuff, so would it be possible for you to make a visit?" [So, in this case] I was real specific about what I wanted—what I needed.

In this case, the project worker was firmly in charge, and directed services provided by other agencies. When the project social worker was asked who would be likely to manage a case, she reinforced the example given above: "Sometimes it seems like it's fifty-fifty, but I think that more likely it would be ourselves as opposed to another agency." When asked the same question, the project director confirmed this statement: "I think we would be seen as the continuity, that we would be the ones who were there all the time and who had the information on the situation."

In terms of formal coordination, Worcester staff did not rely on the existence of written agreements with other agencies. One formal mechanism was attempted: a Crisis Intervention Task Force involving fifteen agencies that occasionally met to advise the staff. According to project and other agency staff, this task force played at most a small role in ongoing case coordination.

The Worcester project was also not likely to call formal case conferences. The social worker reported: "We have had case conferences . . . but that is not usual. Ordinarily, we just conference back and forth on the phone." The director supported this, noting that "most of it is ad hoc . . . , much of it is on the telephone." This is again characteristic of the resources the Worcester project had at its disposal; with few exceptions (such as home health care) staff could offer a host of services on their own. Interagency coordination could therefore take place on a more "ad hoc" basis than in the other two projects.

8

Syracuse: A Service Coordination Model

THE Elder Abuse Project in Syracuse operated as part of a special program within Catholic Charities of Syracuse. This was Alliance, a child abuse and neglect intervention service. Alliance employs a distinct and innovative model for handling child abuse cases and has received national attention due to the effectiveness of its approach. The elder abuse project was based on the Alliance model. In order to describe the model project, it is therefore necessary to briefly discuss the Alliance program for abused children.

The Alliance child abuse project was begun in 1972. It serves abused children from infancy to age 18. All referrals are received from the Child Protective Services division of the local office of the New York Department of Social Services, which has legal responsibility to investigate child abuse cases. The Child Protective Services Division contracts with Alliance to coordinate the investigative process. The latter employs "coordinators" to carry out this function. These individuals put together a "team" for each case, which consists of members of all involved agencies and the family.

Alliance serves an almost exclusively coordinative function. Its work is based on the assumption that the community is rich in services for abusive families, but lacks an entity that puts all the various components of the network together in a coherent treatment plan. Local agencies apparently recognize the need for Alliance's coordinating role in child abuse, as none have refused to participate in the project. Each team meets on an average of once a month; at that time, goals set at the previous meeting are assessed, and the activities of each team member discussed. The Alliance coordinator calls the team together and facilitates discussion. Each year, over 4,000 child abuse team meetings take place.

The Syracuse elder abuse project attempted to apply the Alliance model to maltreatment of the aged. The goal of the project was to coordinate the activities of agencies involved with abusive families, rather than to offer new direct services. Project staff established teams for the elder abuse cases, which usually consisted at a minimum of staff from the Public Health Nursing Department and Adult Protective Services.

In spite of similar goals, however, the elder abuse project differed in a number of ways from the Alliance child abuse model. First, New York has a mandatory reporting law for child abuse cases and a formal investigative procedure that must be followed. Child protective services could also employ legal measures to remove children from a home. Further, the law provides immunity for reporters of abuse of children.

A similar legal apparatus did not exist for elder abuse in New York, and the role of the project was therefore less clearly defined. Elder abuse intervention operated on a strictly voluntary basis. If the client or family was resistant, there was little the project worker could do. As one Syracuse staff member explained: "Our way of organizing the community response, and the way you have to involve the older client and the family, is in a way more delicate, and has to be individually tailored." Since no legal weapon could be employed to force entry into a case, the elder abuse workers had to attempt to obtain the family's compliance through persuasion and the development of trust. To be sure, this process also occured in child abuse cases; however, the elder abuse workers did not have similar legal measures to fall back on if all else failed.

The elder abuse model differed from that employed for child abuse in two other ways. First, the team meeting was less likely to include a family member. This was due in part to the physical frailty of the abuse victim (and sometimes the abuser), as well as the lack of legal pressure to force them to attend team meetings. Second, and perhaps because of the factor just described, the elder abuse workers did more direct service work and more home visits: frail elderly persons were simply unable to attend team meetings. The usual pattern was to hold an interagency service team meeting, after which the person most trusted by the client would telephone or make a home visit.

The central component, then, of the Syracuse model was coordination. There was a second aspect of the program that was also extremely important: the use of specially trained aides who visited abused individuals in their homes. Almost from its inception, Alliance employed "parent aides" for child abuse cases. These aides go into abusive homes and act as positive role models for parents, as well as assisting them in household tasks in such a way as to reduce the level of tension in the household.

The elder abuse aides functioned in much the same fashion. All of the elder abuse aides had had long experience as child abuse aides, and therefore were familiar with difficult domestic settings. The aides spent approximately two to four hours per week in the client's home. Their functions included providing friendly visiting, socialization, and advocacy for clients. The aides also worked with the abuser and other family members to provide respite from caregiving and to model more effective ways of communicating.

The interviews with aides showed an extremely high level of commitment to working with the elderly, as well as lengthy experience in dealing with situations of abuse and neglect. The aides described their primary role as that of supporter for the client and role model for the abuser. One noted that: "I talk with the clients, listen to their frustrations, and try to problem-solve." Another reported that "We lend a ready ear when no one else is there to listen." In this role, according to one aide, "We don't think of ourselves as counselors, but as friends who have information about services and some knowledge we can share."

A variety of other services were performed by the aides; in fact, this flexibility was seen by staff in other community agencies as a key to their success. Thus one aide took her elderly client to get her hair done, while another procured a reading light for the older person. Equally important, the aides attempted to establish a relationship with the perpetrator of the abuse or neglect. One aide reported: "At the start, we went in primarily as an advocate for the victim. Now, we kind of ride the fence on a lot of these cases. You're an advocate for the relative, as well as the elderly."

The project aides were universally praised by staff in other community agencies. The aides themselves, however, noted some problems in their intervention. Primarily, their role in child abuse cases was much better defined, due to the legal sanctions available in such cases. One aide asserted: "It's more difficult to work with the elderly. With child abuse, because of the court order, people accept me whether they want me or not. With the elderly you have to get them to accept you." Another aide expanded on this point: "Say someone is withholding medication. If it's a kid, it's reportable, but not with the elderly. Or once, one of my clients had a black eye. With a child, I would have reported it, and somebody would have been in there."

Such problems did not appear to significantly hamper the aides, however, for community agencies all cited their effectiveness. To give an example, one individual asked the interviewer to "put in a plug for the aide service": He differentiated the elder abuse aide from home health aides available through the Public Health Department, and asserted: "When you have a case where the successful resolution of that case is going to involve the acceptance of the aide, and you have a choice between sending in an Alliance elder abuse aide or one from the Health Department, the chances are that the Alliance aide is going to be able to engage the client and get them to accept services."

In reviewing the function of the model, two basic components stand out in the Syracuse model. The first was an emphasis on interagency coordination, highlighted by the construction of a formal service team for most cases. The second was the use of specially trained aides. The importance of both these elements will become clearer in the case description that follows.

Case example

This case was referred to the project by a county Public Health Nurse who characterized the situation as "volatile." The Adult Protective Division of the Department of Social Services screened the case and confirmed the presence of abuse. Following this the elder abuse project coordinator made a visit with the Public Health nurse. The coordinator identified herself as a Catholic Charities worker, and avoided mention of elder abuse. Based on this visit, the coordinator decided to become involved in the case.

The two individuals involved in the abusive relationship were Edna, age 79, and Jack, age 81. They had been married for fifty-three years, and had no children. By their own reports, the marriage had been a difficult one, and became even worse when Edna suffered a severe stroke in the summer of 1981. She spent ten months in a rehabilitation facility, and after her return home the tension in the relationship increased. The coordinator learned that Edna's depression, short temper, and difficult personality were often too much for Jack to handle. On occasion, he struck and pushed her, and regularly withheld food and medication from her. Edna could not accept the new limitations brought on by the stroke; her response was to scream at Jack and threaten him. During arguments, Edna would throw food and objects at Jack, which would anger him even more. It was in such situations that he physically abused his wife. The coordinator observed bruises and abrasions on Edna's face and arms. Jack admitted to having caused "some of them."

Jack was having considerable difficulty adjusting to his wife's dependence on him. He cooked, kept house, shopped, and in general tried to take on the activities his wife could no longer perform. Although he had substantial savings, he refused to purchase services that might ease the situation. This, he felt, would be "a waste of money." The only assistance the couple received were morning and evening visits by a high school student to get Edna out of and into bed.

After acquiring this information, the coordinator called a team meeting, consisting of the Public Health nurse, Edna, Jack, and the high school student. The situation was discussed, and steps were taken to construct an intervention plan for the case. The coordinator then took the lead role in managing the situation. Based on these early meetings, she determined that the following needs were present: socialization for both parties; time apart from one another; home health aide service; elder abuse aide service; and more regular medical care for Edna. An elder abuse aide was offered immediately for four hours per week, and was accepted. A psychiatric evaluation of Edna was also scheduled.

The availability of family and friends was explored, but such informal supports were non-existent. An adult day care center was contacted for Edna, and arrangements made for an access ramp to be built on the house. The psychiatric evaluation team found her "depressed but competent." The depression was severe enough, however, that the day care center did not feel Edna should attend. She cried most of the time she was there. After two days at the center, this service was discontinued.

The most successful aspect of the initial intervention was the elder abuse aide. The aide was introduced by the coordinator, and began to make weekly visits of three to four hours. The aide visited with Edna and Jack individually as well as together, to try to defuse the anger both felt and to reduce fighting. She provided free time for Jack to leave the house, and accompanied Edna to the adult day health center. She also arranged for a hairdresser to come to the house.

The service team met once a week for the following three weeks. The case appeared to have stabilized, and the team was inactive for two months. At that point, the aide and other service providers began to notice new signs of physical abuse, such as bruises and a black eye. The service team met again, and some new measures were implemented. A worker from Adult Protective Services became involved, and Jack agreed to pay for visits from a Public Health nurse.

Edna's health problems began to worsen around this time. Because of Jack's withholding of medications, Edna's glaucoma had gone untreated, and her eyesight had begun to fail. She also developed decubitus ulcers. She would at times beg to be taken out of house permanently, but balked at the idea of a nursing home. Since her husband refused to pay for nursing home care, she would have to be placed on Medicaid, and a lawsuit filed against Jack for payment. The service team met with the Welfare Department and got approval to put through a Medicaid application. However, Edna refused to give final consent to a nursing home placement, asserting that she wanted "to stay with Jack." During this crisis, the service team expanded to include the following individuals: elder abuse project coordinator, elder abuse aide, Adult Protective Services worker, Public Health nurse, home health aide, psychiatrist, internist, County Health Department supervisor, Department of Social Services supervisor, and Edna and Jack.

The crisis was resolved by the service team in the following way. Edna was given more services, which included several nursing visits each week, four hours a day of home health aide service, and a weekly two hour visit by the Elder Abuse aide. These individuals insured that Edna received her medications properly and followed a better diet. She was also treated for depression. The privately hired helper continued to come for two hours in the morning and two in the evening. Jack received some services from the Public Health nurse, who monitored his heart and blood pressure. He also benefited from social contact with the service workers involved with Edna. In addition, the respite care function of the aides allowed him to spend more time out of the house. As a result of all these interventions, the situation stabilized, and physical abuse stopped.

It should be noted that this case was more complicated and difficult to resolve than some other Syracuse EAP cases. It is useful, however, in that it shows the features of the Syracuse model in very clear relief. First, the elder abuse project worker took the lead in case coordination, juggling a dizzying array of services and agencies. Second, the role of the service team is highlighted in this case: regular team meetings proved crucial to the intervention strategy. Finally, the elder abuse aide played an important part, both as paraprofessional counselor to abuser and abused, and as a monitoring agent. It was, in fact, the aide who alerted the team to the recurrence of abuse after the initial resolution.

Client pathway. After referral of a suspected abuse case, project staff coordinated screening visits with either the Adult Protective Unit or the County Health Department. If it was determined that abuse or neglect was a possibility, the elder abuse coordinator conducted a comprehensive assessment. This assessment involved not only a home visit, but also contacts with other persons involved in the client's life. Based on this evaluation, the coordinator determined whether abuse or neglect was present. If neither abuse nor neglect were found, the client was referred to another appropriate agency.

When maltreatment of the elderly person was confirmed, the coordinator convened a team meeting. As noted, this team usually involved, at a minimum, an Adult Protective Services worker and a Public Health nurse. Whenever possible, the abused client and family members were also involved, but this could not always be done. A service plan was developed at the team meeting and was put into effect. An aide was frequently introduced, and the client's relatives referred to a caregiver support group when appropriate. Throughout the remainder of the time the case was active, the team periodically met to reassess the situation. Alterations in the service plan were made as needed. This process continued until the case was resolved.

It is apparent that the coordinative emphasis of the project is its most important feature. Unlike the Massachusetts model, Syracuse workers could not directly authorize a wide range of services. Instead, they were involved in a constant process of negotiation with agencies that *did* have services at their disposal. The success of the model was therefore dependent on its relationships with other agencies.

PROJECT IMPLEMENTATION

The Syracuse application for the project was initiated by the Metropolitan Commission on the Aging (MCOA), the Area Agency on Aging for the Syracuse area. After some consideration, MCOA decided to approach the Alliance program at Catholic Charities of Syracuse, and to propose that they extend their child abuse intervention model to abused elders. MCOA staff felt that elder services in the community were sufficiently developed, but that greater coordination was needed around abuse cases. As the MCOA planner who wrote the application remarked: "We thought at the start that enough services existed in the community. What had to occur was greater coordination of services. We really weren't looking for a service provider as much as a service coordinator or service integrator. The Alliance child abuse model really seems to work."

It may seem surprising that the project was not located in the Adult Protective Services (APS) division of the local Department of Social Services. APS has formal legal responsibility for intervening in cases of adult maltreatment. In fact, MCOA staff met with personnel at APS before writing the application. Although the APS supervisors were aware of the problem, they noted that only about ten elder abuse cases per year were seen by the agency, and felt that the staff might not be fully sensitive to elder abuse. This was reflected in the comments of an APS supervisor: "We have 27 workers and get 700 referrals a month. Generally, we haven't been able to focus on elder abuse as a problem. We haven't been able to separate it out and to say that these are a group of elder abuse cases, and let's track them and monitor them and keep them separate from all the cases we're involved in. What the project really added was the ability to reach out to elder abuse cases as a group."

Besides the perceived strengths of the Alliance Model, and the belief that it could be applied to elder abuse, respondents also saw strengths in locating the project in Catholic Charities. Many who were interviewed felt that it was advantageous to have more than one place that abused elders or those concerned about them could call. One APS worker agreed: "Welfare has a stigma, especially to the elderly. Being involved with Catholic Charities, the project gets more acceptance. We've referred cases to them for just that reason, knowing that someone in our department isn't going to be welcome."

Yet another advantage of locating the project in Catholic Charities was its religious affiliation. Syracuse is a predominantly Catholic community, and, as one respondent commented, "the elderly are heavily represented in the church-going population." Further, Catholic Charities sponsors meal sites and neighborhood centers, as well as parish outreach workers who funneled clients into the project. Thus, although there may have been mild misgivings about locating an elder abuse project in a child abuse agency (Alliance) the overarching organization of Catholic Charities counterbalanced such concerns by its wide range of elderly services.

The implementation phase of the project went very smoothly because of the internal structure of Catholic Charities and the connection to MCOA. Internally, there were no other workers with whom the project could possibly compete. Other agencies, such as the County Health Department (the major provider of home health care) and the Department of Social Services, already had strong working relationships with Alliance. Public Health nurses and APS workers were accustomed to being on teams coordinated by Alliance Staff. In general, conflict did not occur with other agencies, in the words of the MCOA planner, "because elder abuse wasn't their turf." As will be apparent in the next chapter, relations with APS units in other locations are not always so smooth; more difficulties were experienced in Rhode Island.

As just noted, the tie to MCOA was also of great importance in ensuring the successful implementation of the project. Like EHC, MCOA is the central elder services agency in the region. It funds programs in many other agencies, and thus has a certain amount of leverage over them. MCOA convened a regular monthly meeting of all its subcontracting agencies, at which the programs of each organization were reviewed. This provided an excellent way for the new project to enter the service system.

In discussing the replicability of the Model Project, the director of Alliance stated: "The agency selected [for an elder abuse program] would have to have some clout. We had the coordination label already with hospitals and others, and Catholic Charities has a long service history . . . Any agency would have to have some drawing point and power point to get people to work with them."

By all accounts, the combination of MCOA's high community profile and Alliance's long history of coordinating other service providers gave the project such a "drawing point." It is likely that the success of the Syracuse project was in part due to the strength of this partnership. This was reflected in the virtual lack of serious intra- or interagency implementation problems.

INTERAGENCY COORDINATION

The Syracuse project paid the most extensive attention to issues of interagency coordination. As noted, the project was based on the assumption that a sufficient quantity and variety of elderly services existed in the region, and that what was needed was greater coordination. The Syracuse project was the only one that established a formal structure for coordination: the "team meeting." Coordinative issues were thus of central concern to Syracuse workers.

The project took advantage of numerous formal opportunities for interaction with other agencies. As noted, MCOA sponsored regular monthly meetings of all of its contracting agencies, at which elder abuse cases (among other issues) could be discussed. The agencies involved included an information and referral service, transportation providers, respite care programs, shared housing sites, neighborhood outreach workers, and others. As one participant described it, "This is an informal way of having everybody know what everybody else is doing." The project director echoed this sentiment: "MCOA has a well-organized service system of its own, so there was an immediate, on-going vehicle for us to plug into."

As in Worcester, the project director conducted extensive outreach to other agencies at the beginning of the grant. An advisory committee was established early on, and the agencies represented agreed to refer cases to the project. Further, the director reported, "I went around and talked with people, both administration and line staff. I would ask them to tell me about cases. Then [we] began to intervene in some cases."

Turf issues did not develop with other agencies. The director related that "working with community organizations, like senior centers, I and R, and housing, wasn't a problem. Elder abuse isn't their turf." She raised a very important issue, however, which could have been a major stumbling block for the program: "The Adult Protective Unit in DSS could have been a problem. DSS *is* giving up some power, by allowing us to step in on their turf." As in Rhode Island, the potential for conflict existed between an elder abuse project and adult protective services. An answer must be found to the question: What does a specialized elder abuse program offer that adult protective service does not? If the APS unit did not accept the project, and—as was the case here—no law existed that required reporting, the operation of the project could be very difficult.

In fact, the relationship between APS and the project was excellent. In part, this may be due to the concerted attempt that was made to involve APS staff in planning for the project at its very beginning. It is also partially the result of a history of APS-Alliance collaboration on child abuse cases. Primarily, however, the success of the relationship with APS (and other agencies) lay in the flexibility of the approach of the project, and in the willingness of the staff to adopt different roles depending on the case. It is important to recall that the Syracuse project had neither the legal mandate of the Rhode Island project, nor the range of direct services of the Worcester project. In order to secure interagency cooperation, project staff had to fill a role that served other agencies, while not antagonizing them.

The success of this approach is evident from interviews with APS staff. First, one APS supervisor asserted that the project workers had made great attempts to get to know the front-line APS workers: "Probably just about every supervisor and worker [in this agency] has at one time had some cases in common with [the project staff]. When they walk in everybody knows who they are, and they seem to know all of our people by name. So it's not only on an official, impersonal basis, but we know them and they know us, and if we want to share information or pick their brains, we're not above calling them, and certainly they are not above calling us."

Further, APS staff used the project because of the special training of the workers themselves: "Both [project workers] have extensive backgrounds, and we look to them as people who are into a very specialized area, and who have some competence and proficiency. They know their way around pretty good. And in the cases we carry cooperatively, it gives us a good feeling that we're not in there alone. We can check out our perceptions and share our ideas. All in all, it's nice to have another agency in there working with you. Sometimes by carrying out specific work roles on that case, you get things done that we probably wouldn't otherwise."

Thus, the major potential conflict was defused through mutual acceptance and coordinated planning. Without providing additional examples, other agencies uniformly supported this view of the Syracuse Project. In fact, the project was actually able on occasion to defuse conflict between other agencies; they stepped in, for example, on a disagreement between APS and Public Health Nursing and helped to resolve it.

One major reason for the positive response towards the project on the part of other agencies was its great degree of flexibility with regard to case management. In theory, the project was expected to play a primary management role, as it was based on coordination. However, the project staff in actual practice adopted a wide range of case management styles, from assuming direct responsibility for the case to acting as an occasional consultant.

This flexibility is evident in the area of referrals. The project director reported that APS and the project "work side by side; people can call where they feel the most comfortable." An APS supervisor echoed this sentiment: "Perhaps it was important with the Health Department that they have two places they could send a referral, and if they didn't think [APS] was moving with the speed they wanted, or in the direction they wanted, they could probably say 'well damn them, I'm going to send this over to Elder Abuse.' "

Similarly, the on-going management of elder abuse cases is highly flexible; so much so, that respondents even had a little difficulty identifying who is most likely to have ultimate responsibility. As the director described the process:

> I guess we get a referral and go out on it, often with a Protective Service worker, sometimes alone, sometimes with someone else, and make an assessment and be responsible for sitting down at a meeting, trying to work out who's going to do what; and who's going to sell the family on this plan. Then we make some attempt to keep on track. If there is an APS worker that has a relationship and can continue to stay involved, we really would not seek much direct contact. Ideally, the way the coordination role would go would be to go in on the assessment process, have a direct hands-on and a chance to observe and form an opinion, and then [all the agencies involved] would share that and come to some agreement with help from DSS as to what our roles would be. Then from time to time we would convene things . . . but some of that wasn't done in a meeting. We don't follow as formal a structure as the Alliance Child Abuse teams. We might be more likely to get on the phone. If there seems to be some reason to get Protective Services and Public Health Nursing and ourselves back together for a sit-down, we would.

It was apparent from comments such as these that the coordinating role of the Syracuse staff was allowed to vary according to a number of factors, including the primary nature of the problem and who first discovered the case. In this way, it is unlike the Worcester project, which generally assumed case management responsibility for its clients. Worcester staff had such strong control over services that they became the logical coordinator for other agencies involved in the case. Syracuse staff were often placed in an official coordination role (for example, they might call a team meeting), but on-going, day-to-day monitoring was as likely as not to be carried out by another agency.

In conclusion, the Syracuse project was found to have had no serious problems in interagency coordination. The interviews showed great appreciation for the project on the part of other agencies. They also demonstrated a high degree of flexibility on the part of project staff as to the way in which responsibility was shared. Formal and informal mechanisms of coordination appear to have been firmly established, and to have functioned smoothly.

9

Rhode Island: Mandatory Reporting Model

THE Rhode Island Model Project was located in the Department of Elderly Affairs (DEA), which is the state agency with primary responsibility for meeting the needs of elderly residents. It serves the entire state, and receives federal, state, and local funding. Six months after the inception of the Model Project, the Rhode Island General Assembly enacted a mandatory elder abuse reporting law. This law maintained that DEA receive reports, carry out an investigation of suspicious cases, and coordinate with other service providers.

Thus, Rhode Island was the only Model Project that operated under a mandatory reporting statute. At the risk of oversimplification, this legal responsibility was the core element of the Rhode Island project. The coordinating and counseling activities performed by the project staff were shaped by the fact that it was a statewide project operating within a state agency, under mandatory reporting.

Some of the effects of this situation were noted by the project staff. The Rhode Island model had a primarily short-term focus and relied on extensive coordination with other agencies to provide on-going direct services. The major roles of the project were to act as a catalyst for intervention and to conduct investigations. When suspected cases of abuse and neglect were referred to DEA, project staff were required to initiate an investigation within twenty-four hours. Staff investigated and assessed each case, and attempted to establish a care plan in cooperation with other agencies.

This mandatory reporting aspect becomes clearest in the comments of other agencies on the project. When asked why she might contact the Project, a social worker from another agency responded: "Because DEA has the mandate to investigate and coordinate services the way the law is written. So it's a matter of following the law. We certainly want to provide what's best for the client, but we do so after checking it out with DEA, or in consultation with them, or at their request, because of the way the law is written."

A worker at a senior center, in answer to the same question, replied: "It's the central point to report incidents." The response of a social work consultant from a home health agency shows this formal responsibility even more clearly: she would report cases, but try to keep the project staff from intervening. Her concern was with fulfilling the letter of the law. She stated: "What I find is, in a few cases, when we make the report, I'm already working with the nurse on it. By the time the nurse feels something is going on, she already has a good relationship with the person, and so a lot of times I'll report to the elder abuse project but I'll say 'Don't go in . . .' I tend to report all suspected cases . . . but I feel comfortable asking them not to go out."

In this case, perhaps most clearly, the project was seen as the official recipient of calls, rather than as an integral part of an intervention strategy. Another respondent echoed this; when asked if she would report a case to the project if the law did not exist, she replied: "We wouldn't feel so bound. We use the program to a large extent because of the law."

Another important difference between the Rhode Island project and the other two was its lack of ability to directly authorize services to clients. Certain services were available in other components of the DEA, including information and referral, long-term care ombudsman, homemaker/home health aides (for financially eligible clients), and senior companions. The project staff did not, however, have *direct* control over these services. Unlike the Worcester model, Rhode Island project workers could not personally authorize services.

With this emphasis on the project's legal responsibility in mind, and its lack of direct services, it is possible to review other basic features of the model. When suspected cases of abuse and neglect were referred to the project, the staff were required to investigate within twenty-four hours. These referrals were first screened by information and referral (I and R) workers. According to the director of the I and R service, the screening was generally straightforward, as callers usually specified that they were reporting abuse or neglect. He noted: "The elder abuse program is visible, so most of the people have a pretty clear idea of why they're calling.

It's very rare that a person asks about one thing, and then, in a long conversation, you find abuse is going on, too."

After preliminary screening, the I and R worker referred cases of abuse and neglect to the elder abuse team. Ideally, all new cases were to go to the social worker, rather than the Model Project administrator. In reality, the administrator developed a caseload of her own. This was in part due to the fact that the original social worker left the project after approximately one year and the administrator had to take on cases until a new one was hired. In addition to cases which came in through the I and R unit, both staff members received referrals directly from agency staff who were acquainted with them. Workers in other community agencies often prefered to circumvent the I and R unit and speak directly with Model Project staff.

The Model Project social worker summed up the next steps in case intervention as follows:

> After I receive a complaint of abuse, with the information I have, I decide what my next step will be. If there are other agencies involved, I'll call them. If there are family members involved, I'll call them. If it's a physical violence case or a matter of personal safety, I immediately go to visit the home.

She continued:

> After an I and R referral, I will call whatever numbers are on the I and R form. If the person is on SSI, say, I know they must have a social worker, so I'll call the Department of Social and Rehabilitative Services [agency that administers welfare program]. Before I go to the house, I try to get as much information as I can. For example, when I went to one case where the husband and wife were beating on each other, I stopped at the police station first to see if they knew of them. They said it had been going on for six years. So I do a little investigation prior to going in to the home. Unless it's an emergency; then I just go.

The emphasis in this service model is *investigation*: the project had the responsibility to determine if abuse occured and, if it had, to try to set a treatment plan in motion. Staff occasionally served in a coordinating role, but to a much more limited extent then in the other Model Projects. When asked whether other agencies look to the project for coordination, the abuse project social worker responded:

> Sometimes. But sometimes it would be very inappropriate. For example, in one case I was one of the people involved, but the person who organized meetings with the family was the nurse there. It was appropriate because that was her community and they all knew each other.

She added:

> Every case is different. You have to assess the resources, assess the roles, and assess your role constantly in each case. It's usually very evident what your role should be . . . sometimes you lay back and function as a part of it; sometimes you get the people together.

Because of the mandatory reporting law, project staff were informed of the case, but frequently did not take a major case management role in it. In the other Model Projects, a call to staff was generally a request for heavy involvement and probable on-going case management.

Another aspect of the project was the usually short-term involvement project staff had in cases. The project social worker was asked whether an attempt was made to get other agencies to take over the primary responsibility for a case quickly. She replied:

> "Yes. They have to. My primary responsibility is to investigate the abuse, and through whatever means I can—peaceful at first, negotiating second, and by legal means and threats last of all, to eliminate the abuse . . . when other agencies take over, we tend to withdraw."

Other agencies substantiated this point; the Model Project was seen as having a short-term, investigative focus.

There were two major reasons for this aspect of the Model Project. The first has already been noted: unlike the other two projects, Rhode Island staff had no direct access to services. The Worcester project could authorize a wide range of services, and Syracuse at least could make specialized aides available. Because of the lack of access to services, in Rhode Island other agencies took over the coordinating function as a natural outgrowth of their direct service activities.

Second, the Rhode Island project received a massive number of referrals: over 400 over the course of the demonstration. Staff were clearly unable to have an intensive involvement in each case. In order to carry out an investigation of each call, they were required to delegate major portions of the day-to-day intervention to other agencies. As a Social and Rehabilitative Service supervisor noted: "We see them as having the mandate and the authority to do something, and we want them to know what's going on. But a lot of the day-to-day stuff we do ourselves. They couldn't do it, because of their limited staffing."

It is interesting to note that the project even delegated the investigative process to other agencies in some cases. As the project director reported: "We must investigate. But the investigation can take many different forms." According to the director:

It would be impossible for us to go into any home on a one-time basis and be able to find out all the ramifications of that case, and if you've got a direct service person who's been going in to see this person over time, they definitely would have a lot more information than we ever would. So that our best advantage is to find out from them and coordinate with them. We depend on other agencies, like Social and Rehabilitative Services, VNA's, or the police, to do valid assessment.

The key features of the Rhode Island Model Project, then, appear to be shaped by its role as the legally designated agency to receive reports of elder abuse. The project was aided by other agencies extensively in both the investigation and intervention stages, and it delegated responsibility whenever possible. It did not characteristically carry clients over the long term, but relied on other agencies for this. The project was usually only contacted again if abuse reemerged as a major problem.

Case example

Mary, a woman in her late seventies who was in the early stages of Alzheimer's disease, lived with her son Joe and his wife Sally. Although the arrangement had been fairly free of problems, Mary's other son, Fred, wished to assume caregiving responsibilities, and Joe acceded to his wishes. Fred and his wife Louise were not good caretakers, however. Mary was moved to a small room in the basement, and was cut off from interaction with Fred's family. She was lonely and frightened.

Mary attended a day care center, where she described the problems in her home. The day care staff contacted a local senior center, which in turn contacted the elder abuse project. The project social worker learned that Mary was receiving home health care, and contacted the supervising nurse who was familiar with the case. A meeting was set up between the project worker, the home health nurse, a nurse from the day care center, and the director of the senior center.

As these individuals compared notes, they rapidly came to the conclusion that, as the project social worker stated, "something funny was going on." They decided that Mary was in danger, in particular because she would be unable to escape in the event of a fire. In addition, they felt the situation was psychologically damaging, as evidenced by Mary's reluctance to leave the van when she came home from the day care center. Finally, one of the home health aides who worked with the case reported to the nurse that Mary had been pushed by the daughter-in-law.

The strategy decided upon at this meeting was to relocate Mary to a nursing home. The project social worker met with Joe and Sally, who agreed that a nursing home would be the best option. The worker attempted to help them deal with guilt feelings about this decision. A home visit was never made by the project social worker, who felt it would "disrupt the family system." Instead, she met with Mary at the day care center. This process of meeting with relevant parties took approximately five weeks, after which all parties—including Fred and Louise—agreed on nursing home placement. After placement, project staff continued follow-up with the client for a time.

In broad outline, this case shows some basic features of the Rhode Island project. It had a primarily short-term focus, and relied on other agencies to provide direct services and monitor cases. The role of the elder abuse project was to serve as a central point for reports, and to take official responsibility for the investigation process. Other agencies reported contacting the project because the law required them to, and not because they desired assistance from the project.

Client pathway. Cases came in to Rhode Island DEA through the I and R unit, which conducted preliminary screening of the case. If the I and R worker suspected abuse or neglect, it was referred to the project. The Director determined how urgent the case was, and then transferred it to the social worker. After an initial assessment, a decision was made as to whether the project should manage the case; questions of cooperativeness and competency of the client were influential in this decision. Regardless of which agency took primary responsibility, project staff attempted to monitor the progress of each case until it was resolved. Unfortunately, limited staffing made this monitoring function sometimes very difficult.

PROJECT IMPLEMENTATION

The Rhode Island project was located in the Department of Elderly Affairs due to a convergence of factors. In a sense, DEA was in competition to a degree with the state's welfare department (the Department of Social and Rehabilitative Services), which provides adult protective services. In

1979, both DEA and SRS proposed legislation for elder protective services, and both were voted down. In the following year, however, a mandatory reporting law was passed that made DEA the designated agency to respond to reports of abuse.

During the same period, the Mental Health Coordinator of DEA had become aware of increasing concern regarding elder abuse. In concert with the DEA director, she applied for the AOA Model Project demonstration funds, which were granted. This serendipitous turn of events placed the project in an unusual situation: its staff became responsible for abuse investigation under mandatory reporting.

Unlike the other two sites, consensus did not exist among respondents that DEA was the best location for the Model. According to one SRS worker: "Our agency has a mechanism in place [to handle abuse]. I suspect that it's a political issue. This project could function as well in SRS. It would handle it, because the mechanism is there. For instance, it would be more geographically feasible [at SRS] than the way it's operated out of here." Other interviewees concurred that the project could be as or more effectively located in SRS.

Some positive aspects of the DEA location were noted, however. DEA was acknowledged to have good public relations expertise, and to have mounted an effective awareness campaign among the elderly. Further, DEA, as a state agency, was perceived as having "clout" with recalcitrant individuals. As a VNA nurse noted, DEA involvement was useful in "situations when families are scattered and unresponsive. When DEA goes in and calls them together, they tend to straighten up." This observation was echoed by a social worker in a senior center: "Being from DEA has clout. Just the fact that DEA is involved has changed the behavior of some family members, and made it easier for the VNA to go in, or for me to go in."

The desirability of the project's location was thus somewhat more ambiguous in Rhode Island. Unlike Syracuse and Worcester, the major advantage was seen as a negative one: when all else failed, DEA could go in. As will be discussed in a later section, the project's lack of a direct service component appears to be a major reason for this attitude.

Because of mandatory reporting, DEA was spared a problem initially encountered (albeit to a relatively slight degree) at the other two sites: case-finding. The Rhode Island project was quickly inundated with referrals. Because of the legal sanctions against nonreporting, other agencies were only too willing to refer cases to the project. Perhaps for this reason, the project focused much of its outreach attempts not on other agencies, but on elderly persons themselves. A major vehicle in this effort was a series of skits on elder abuse that were performed widely to senior citizen's groups around the state.

INTERAGENCY COORDINATION

Rhode Island, like the other two Model Projects, employed both formal and informal mechanisms of coordination. A major formal entity were the "key councils" established by the Rhode Island DEA. These are interagency groups of service providers that meet at regular intervals. A special subcommittee of the Providence (R.I.) Key Council was established to work specifically with the project. Rhode Island staff also conducted information sessions with local agencies, although, as noted above, most of the outreach was targeted toward elderly people themselves.

Based on the interviews, the Rhode Island project appeared to have more difficulties in interagency coordination than did the other two. Other agencies were more likely to express dissatisfaction with the coordinative process, and to see a need for mechanisms that would make interagency interaction smoother. It is of great importance to this analysis that the reasons behind such problems in coordination *lie in the basic structure of the model.* That being so, they have critical implications for the replicability of the Rhode Island model.

As described earlier, the Rhode Island project has two noteworthy facets. First, it was the only project that operated under the constraints of mandatory reporting. As such, it received more referrals than the other projects; many more, in fact, than could have been successfully casemanaged by the staff. Therefore, an attempt was made to transfer control of cases to other agencies as quickly as possible. Second, Worcester and Syracuse had concrete services to offer—Worcester, a wide range of home care services, and Syracuse, specialized case aides. The Rhode Island project, however, had to rely on other agencies for help, in exchange for which, because of time constraints, they had little to offer in return.

Other agencies reported that they usually contacted DEA because the law required them to do so. But they generally recognized that it was difficult for elder abuse project staff to involve themselves extensively in any individual case. As one interviewee noted:

[The project staff] have taken on a lot. They have to cover a large geographical area. They are doing a lot of running around, and I wonder if it isn't a situation that's brought on just by the structure, the nature of the program. The law puts them in a difficult situation, because while it mandates that they investigate certain types of abuse and neglect . . . and provide services. There are just not enough services out there for them to resolve situations quickly.

A staff person from another agency also highlighted the constraints on the time of the project staff: "when they weren't too busy, they wanted to be in charge of cases. When they got busy, they wanted to push cases over to community agencies."

As might be inferred from these comments, the project was considered by many agencies to be unlikely to take on direct management of a case. Referrals were made to comply with the law, and occasionally the "clout" of the state agency would be employed, but on the whole, other agencies would attempt to stay in charge. An Adult Protective Services worker reported:

> If we have a case they've seen, but decided no action is appropriate, we monitor it. If we see it approaching a crisis state, we call DEA and say we think the case is going to blow. We see them as having mandate and having the authority to do something, and want them to know what's going on. But a lot of the day-to-day stuff we do ourselves. DEA couldn't do the day-to-day stuff because of staffing.

When asked if the Model Project had changed her agency's way of handling abuse cases, she went on:

> No, [before the project] we would handle it in the same way, except we wouldn't call in, and we wouldn't have another agency to work with . . . our procedure hasn't changed at all.

Thus, the design of the project caused it to give responsibility for cases to other agencies, and to rely on them for help in managing the case. However, other agencies perceived the project as having little to offer in return in the way of needed direct services. It also was unable to take problem cases off other agencies' hands in a permanent way, unlike the Worcester project. For this reason, an imbalanced exchange existed between the project and other agencies. This was evident even when the interviewee expresseed overall satisfaction with the project. For example, a social worker from a senior center who in general spoke highly of the project noted that of the four times he had made joint visits with the project worker, *he* had never initiated the contact. Instead, project staff had called him for help.

In order to shed additional light on the Rhode Island project, it is useful to present findings from the Organizational Assessment Instrument. It will be recalled that the agencies identified by each project as its primary contacts were given an OAI questionnaire. This instrument contained a variety of questions regarding interaction and satisfaction with the project. As noted earlier, five agencies were identified by Rhode Island and Worcester and four by Syracuse. Generally, this analysis uncovered broader similarities between the Worcester and Syracuse projects than between either of those projects and Rhode Island. In particular, other agencies were more likely to report imbalanced exchange with the Rhode Island project.

Agencies in all three sites felt that they were quite or very well acquainted with the elder abuse staff. In subsequent questions, however, differences were found. Other agencies in Rhode Island were less likely to feel that they were very well informed about the project; that effective working relationships existed with the project; and that the give-and-take relationship with the project was mutual. They were more likely to report that the Rhode Island project needed *their* services or support.

Worcester and Syracuse were both more apt than Rhode Island to have verbal and written understandings with other agencies. Rhode Island agencies reported greater frequency of disagreements with the project, and were less likely to feel that such disagreements were successfully worked out. Syracuse agencies felt the most strongly that the project was important to them in attaining their own goals, while Rhode Island agencies reported this the least.

Syracuse agencies also were most likely to feel the relationship with the Model Project was productive and that their effort spent developing and maintaining this relationship was worthwhile. Agencies in Worcester registered the most overall satisfaction with the project. Rhode Island lagged behind the other two projects in these areas. As our previous discussion indicates, these difficulties appear to be related to the mandatory reporting statute's impact on the Rhode Island project.

SUMMARY

We have discussed interagency coordination in Rhode Island at such length because such coordination was even more critical to this project than for Syracuse or Worcester, due to the nature of the model. Worcester controlled many services in its own agency, and Syracuse provided the important aide service. Rhode Island was not seen as offering anything like this, so, in order to succeed, it would have been necessary to maintain productive relationships with other agencies. Instead, an imbalance of exchange was found.

One major way of remedying this imbalance would have been the inclusion of a direct services component in the Rhode Island project; that is, services that project staff could have personally authorized to help other agencies. The problem appears to be one of lack of resources; the establishment of a Syracuse-type aide program could have been a first possible step to overcome this problem.

Further, a decentralization of the program into local agencies would probably have been advisable. The staff were too severely taxed by the sheer number of very serious referrals. Trained workers could have been placed in local agencies under the general supervision of the project staff. Previous research has shown the need for specialized abuse workers, which would recommend against shifting investigative responsibility to regular community agency staff. If some agencies were to employ part- or full-time workers to intervene in cases after they were reported to the Model Project, a more comprehensive response would become possible.

It is important to note that Rhode Island DEA staff became aware that some agencies were resistant to DEA intervention and took steps to overcome coordination problems. First, DEA moved to make clear to its grantee agencies that the funding they received was in part to cover case management of abuse cases. Contracts with senior centers and social service agencies became more specific in this way. The relationship between the department and its grantee agencies, DEA staff reported, was strengthened due to this clarification of DEA's expectations regarding the role of these agencies in case management for abuse victims.

Second, monthly meetings were held for workers involved in abuse cases. These meetings were scheduled and conducted by DEA staff and provided an opportunity for workers to express their concerns, share their difficulties, and receive ongoing training. Sessions for this group were held with the Attorney General's Office regarding legal issues, with mental health professionals regarding commitment procedures, and with a legal services developer regarding probate court. According to DEA, these sessions proved to be very valuable, keeping the lines of communication open between workers and DEA staff. Thus, at the close of the evaluation, the project was working to overcome some of the difficulties described in this chapter.

PART FOUR

Realities and Recommendations

10

Helping Elderly Victims: What the Model Projects Have Taught Us

I N this final chapter, we draw together the major findings of the Model Projects study and discuss the most important implications of the research. It begins with a summary of the results about the nature of elder abuse and neglect. We then offer some insights into the replicability of the Model Projects, future research, and policy and practice issues.

THE NATURE OF ELDER ABUSE AND NEGLECT

Using uniform data collection instruments, information was obtained about 328 victims and their families over a two-year period. The victims were most likely to be female, in their mid-seventies, and living in a household with family members. They tended to have some difficulties with instrumental activities of daily living and were in poor emotional health. Although they were sometimes dependent on their relatives for assistance in such areas of daily living as transportation, and companionship, they were relatively independent in terms of financial resources.

The perpetrators tended to be male and to suffer from psychological problems. They were apt to be dependent on the victims for economic support. A significant number of the perpetrators had a history of mental illness and alcohol abuse and had experienced a recent decline in their mental state. Their lives were stressful, sometimes from the demands of the victim, but more often from their own mental and physical health problems, or from financial problems. Social contacts appeared to be minimal for a substantial proportion of the sample.

The most common form of maltreatment was psychological abuse, followed by physical and material abuse, then passive and active neglect. For a large proportion of victims, the mistreatment was quite serious, involving multiple manifestations. The abuse situations had usually existed for over a year, and in some cases had gone on for decades.

To learn more about the circumstances surrounding elder abuse and neglect, we carried out three analyses involving subgroups of the sample: the first compared the characteristics of five types of abuse and neglect; the second contrasted cases of abuse of spouses with abuse of parents; and the third involved in-depth interviews with a group of physically abused elders.

In the first analysis, we found that cases of physical abuse were more likely to involve victims and perpetrators in poor emotional health. The victims, in spite of emotional problems, were generally independent in most areas of daily living. On the other hand, the perpetrators were apt to abuse alcohol, to have a history of mental illness and to have undergone a recent decline in both mental and physical health status. In this type of maltreatment, it was the perpetrator who had experienced an increase in dependency. A generally similar pattern existed for psychological abuse.

A somewhat different profile was presented by the material abuse cases. This form of abuse was motivated by the financial needs of the perpetrators, who were more likely to have long-term and recent financial problems and to have undergone a change in their financial or job status. Alcohol abuse was also a significant factor in this group. The relative social isolation of victims may have played a role; material abuse victims were more apt to be unmarried and to have suffered losses in their social network. The perpetrators were generally distant relatives or non-relatives who were not as emotionally involved with their victims as were other abusers.

In marked contrast to the physical or psychological abuse cases, those involving neglect appeared to be related to the dependency needs of the victim. Neglected older persons had significant problems with cognitive and physical functioning that forced them to depend on their caretakers for assistance with many activities of daily living. Because of their infirmities and advanced age, they were more likely to be a source of stress to their relatives. The perpetrators were not as financially dependent on their victims or as beset with mental problems as the perpetrators of physical or material abuse. Social isolation was a contributing factor since there was evidence of a loss of social supports in cases of passive neglect and a lack of emergency contact for victims of active neglect.

When we compared elders who were victimized by spouses with those victimized by children, we found that spouses tended to be physically abused, to be in poorer emotional health, and to be more dependent on the perpetrators for companionship, financial resources and management, and maintenance of property. The spouse perpetrators were more likely to have had both long-term and recent medical complaints and to have had a recent decline in their health status. In some older marriages, the stability in the relationship achieved through a series of adjustments over a lifetime may be compromised by stressful events, such as the declining physical and emotional health of either one or both parties. External stress may upset the delicate balance of a vulnerable marriage and lead to anger, hostility and abuse.

Among parent abuse cases, the victims were more apt to be exploited and psychologically abused. A significantly larger proportion of adult-child perpetrators had a history of mental illness and alcoholism and were financially dependent on their victims. For these perpetrators, life was more stressful. Some had both long-term and recent financial difficulties or had been through a recent divorce or separation. Their lives were also more lonely: a substantially larger proportion had no social contacts.

These adult children had difficulty managing their own lives, either because of a history of mental illness, alcoholism or poor emotional state. They have been unsuccessful in their marriages, jobs, and social relationships. Although they may provide some assistance to their elderly parents by virtue of being in the same household, they often need the parent more than the parent needs them.

The third analysis attempted to overcome some of the validity and reliability problems inherent in the study. Specifically, since the project staff were responsible for completing the assessment forms, the information that they provided reflected their perception and program orientation. Although attempts were made to insure intra-site reliability by limiting data collection for each project to the two staff persons who were most familiar with the cases and who were trained in the use of the instruments, agreement under the circumstances was difficult to achieve.

The in-depth analysis of selected physical abuse cases was designed to correct this deficiency. The clients were interviewed directly by one researcher, and standardized scales were used to measure functional status, health, stress, social support, and a number of other areas. The similarity in the findings for the physical abuse cases by the two research methods suggests that, despite the methodological shortcomings of the case assessment procedure described above, the latter did produce reliable results.

Forty-two elderly physical abuse victims were compared to a matched nonabused control group. The abusers were much more likely than the control relatives to have mental or emotional problems, to abuse alcohol, and to have been hospitalized for psychiatric reasons. The results on the dependency variables indicated that abused elders were not less healthy or more functionally disabled than the control group; in fact, they were less disabled in a number of areas. The victims were not more dependent on their kin than the comparisons for assistance with activities of daily living, but the perpetrators were more likely to be dependent on their elderly relatives than were the control relatives. In addition, the victims were found to have fewer social contacts and to be less satisfied with those they did have.

What is to be learned from these analyses regarding the nature of elder abuse and neglect? First, it is clear that mistreatment of the elderly is not a phenomenon that can be explained by a single theory or treated by a certain procedure. Rather it consists of multiple manifestations that represent particular responses to the dynamics within the family, and to a lesser extent, the social and cultural forces of the larger environment. By taking into account the distinctive qualities associated with the various types of mistreatment and the victims and perpetrators, intervention projects can refine their approaches to victims.

A second important finding of the study is the emergence of psychopathology of the perpetrator as an important risk factor. Contrary to the minor role that it is currently given in the family violence literature, psychopathology appears to be a major explanatory variable for elder abuse. There is, of course, the possibility that the significance of the variable might be a methodological artifact: cases reported to community agencies might be more psychopathological than those found in the general community. However, the prevalence survey conducted subsequently by Finkelhor and Pillemer (1987) has confirmed the importance of deviance of the perpetrator as a factor in physical abuse and verbal aggression.

Third, material abuse emerged from the study as a distinct phenomenon. The perpetrator was less likely to be a close relative of the victim. Except in cases where it was used as retaliation for earlier familial or marital conflicts, material abuse appears to be motivated by desire for financial gain and may be better understood and treated by viewing it as a criminal act.

Fourth, the special analysis of data obtained directly from physically abused older persons leads to a general point: The theories of elder abuse that relate to the problems of the abuser, and to the relationship between abuser and victim were generally supported. Significantly less support was found for more "social structural" causes of violence. To sociologists, the dearth of findings that validate a social structural approach to the causation of elder abuse may be disturbing. The evidence is consistent, however.

Thus, the "cycle of violence" theory was not supported here; that is, there did not appear to be a connection in this sample between physical abuse experienced as a child and committing acts of elder abuse. It was noted in chapter 2 that the existence of such a cycle would lead credence to social learning theory, which holds that the family is the "cradle of violence." From the evidence we have presented, the early family lives of the abusers do not appear to have been unusually violent. Further, the other sociocultural factors—chronic economic strain and stressful life events—played only a small role in the abuse situations. The sociocultural theory may not offer the explanatory power that has been found with other forms of family violence. Of course, much additional research is needed on this issue.

The fifth point relates to the issue of dependency. Most important, the notion that physical elder abuse results only from the strain of caring for a dependent old person found little support in this study. Instead, we are left with the image of an impaired, dependent perpetrator, who uses physical violence to obtain money or goods, or to compensate for a lack of power in his or her relationship with the victim.

These results make it necessary to question the conventional depiction of elder abuse. It has become fashionable to characterize the families of the elderly as willing, responsible caretakers. This view is due largely to research on caregiving, but also in part because families have come to be seen as a key component in reducing the public costs of long-term care. The resulting perspective taken by many persons interested in elder abuse was one that tended to blame the victim. The elderly, it has been held, are hard to care for. They create stress for their relatives, who in turn get angry, lose control, and abuse or neglect the old person.

Based on the evidence provided by both the case assessment and interview data, we must be willing to shed, or at least suspend, accepted notions about the responsible behavior of some relatives of the elderly. In particular, elder abuse researchers must begin to view the phenomenon more from a domestic violence perspective, rather than as a "caregiving" problem. The finding that a significant proportion of elder mistreatment is perpetrated by spouses lends weight to this argument. The child abuse model, which has guided so many of the initial studies and policies in elder abuse, has little merit as a framework for understanding the dynamics between marital partners or even adult children and their parents.

By arguing that interventions must focus on the perpetrator, we certainly do not wish to return to theories of a "criminal type" to explain deviant behavior such as elder abuse. We do assert, however, that the characteristics of the abuser, rather than those of the old person, may be strongly associated with violence against the elderly. We return below to the policy implications of these findings.

MODEL REPLICABILITY

By the time the demonstration ended, all of the projects had recorded a large decrease in the number of manifestations and degree of severity of the mistreatment, as well as a significant reduction in the level of threat that it posed for the victim. They also made progress in reducing the degree of dependency of both the perpetrator and victim in various activities of daily living and in improving the quality of the relationship between the two parties.

Given the multiplicity and complexity of the problems that the project staff encountered in their cases, some of which involved very troubled and functionally disabled families, the number of cases that they were able to resolve and to help is very encouraging. The results in the three sites indicate improvements in a majority of cases. For more than half the cases, the victims remained in their own homes. These cases particularly tested the skills of the staff in developing a trusting relationship with the family, assessing the situation correctly, and coordinating the services required to keep the family intact.

We must remember, however, that the projects, although similar in goals, target population, staffing, and operational definitions, represented various approaches to elder abuse and neglect intervention. The Worcester project was located in an agency where the caseworkers had the authority to order a wide range of social services; we therefore termed it a "service brokerage" model. The Syracuse project, on the other hand, functioned primarily as a coordinator of services supplied by other agencies and was described as a "coordination" model. It did however, have direct control over a group of aides who worked with the most difficult cases. The Rhode Island project was characterized as a "mandatory reporting" model. Because the agency was authorized to receive reports under a mandatory reporting law, it was forced to respond to a unique set of demands.

Because of the variations in function and structure, the projects faced different problems in developing and implementing their programs, and had different strengths and weaknesses. It is therefore *not* the goal of this analysis to determine whether one project was "better" than another. Such a determination would in fact be impossible, for each project responded to the demands of its environment in a unique way. Without question, all three projects managed as best as they could in often difficult situations, and achieved considerable success. It *is* possible, however, to ask: Is one of the intervention models more easily replicable than the others? Could the basic features of one model be more easily adapted to another community than those of the others? Based on our previous discussion, we would argue that the Syracuse model is the most replicable.

The circumstances of the Worcester and Rhode Island projects were somewhat special. Massachusetts, unlike most other states, has an extensive network of state-funded agencies (Home Care Corporations) that provide case management and social services to all frail elderly persons in the state who meet the eligibility requirements. Because of this unusual comprehensive home care model, it seems unrealistic to recommend the Worcester program as a national model for elder abuse intervention. Simply, comparable service entities frequently do not exist in other locations.

Rhode Island also represents a somewhat special circumstance. As part of the state unit on aging, it had considerable leverage in working with other agencies. Because of Rhode Island's small size, it was possible for the state agency staff to have direct service responsibilities. Of course, such a delivery model would not work in larger states, where elder abuse intervention would have to be decentralized. Further, dissatisfaction with the project was reported by community agencies, due to lack of sufficient staff and other direct services.

Of the three projects, the Syracuse model stands out as the best for communities to consider. Its efforts at coordination of elder abuse cases were extremely well received by community agencies. Using the team conference as a coordination strategy, the Syracuse project was able to involve local service providers—including the Adult Protective Services unit—in the case management process without raising issues of territoriality and conflict. Although it did not have a wide range of services to offer, it did employ a group of aides who could assist in the coordination and monitoring process.

Further, because no special sponsorship is needed, such as a home care corporation or a state or Area Agency on Aging, any well-respected human service organization can adopt the program. This flexibility, as well as the success in case resolution, make the Syracuse project an attractive one for replication. It is in this context that we offer the following suggestions for increasing the likelihood that an elder abuse intervention project will be successful.

GUIDELINES FOR A SUCCESSFUL PROJECT DESIGN

What have we learned from these projects that will assist us in creating new intervention programs, or in redesigning existing ones? Clearly, we can only attempt to answer this question with considerable caution. We would be remiss if we attempted to draw firm conclusions from the case study data available to us. In the absence of other comparative data on elder abuse programs, however, we feel justified in hazarding several recommendations regarding the organization and delivery of services to elder abuse victims and their families.

1. *A need exists for specific elder abuse programs.* In chapter 1, the question was posed: Is there a need for service programs for abused and neglected elders, or should these programs be dealt with in the context of existing service systems? The results of the three Model Projects indicate that specialized interventions for elder abuse victims are indeed necessary. The three projects were inundated with referrals within a relatively short period after opening. Other community agencies perceived a need for assistance from persons with special expertise in handling abuse and neglect cases. Even when staff from agencies felt that they had the ability to deal with such cases, they rarely had sufficient time to manage all of their complexities. In sum, this evaluation indicates that there is in fact much to be gained by creating service programs for elder abuse.

2. *An elder abuse project should be located in, or affiliated with, a high-profile community agency.* All three of the Model Projects benefited greatly from their connection to a well-established agency that was a magnet for services to older persons in the community. The Rhode Island DEA and the Worcester EHC were both seen as the premier service providers to

the aged in their regions. In Syracuse, the model project had the double advantage of being sponsored by the Metropolitan Commission on Aging of Onandaga County (MCOA), well-known for policy and planning leadership, and by Catholic Charities, which had a number of direct service programs. Perhaps most important, DEA, EHC, and MCOA all funded certain other agencies. This allowed them to use their "pull" with grantee agencies to bring referrals and assistance to the elder abuse project. Elder abuse intervention programs seem to work well when the sponsoring agency is seen as having "clout."

3. *An elder abuse project should offer direct services.* One major problem with the Rhode Island project was resentment from other agencies that felt the project had little to offer them. The staff were too busy to be able to entirely take a difficult case off of another agency's hands and did not offer them many new resources to assist them in managing the case. The Worcester and Syracuse projects, on the other hand, both had important direct services to offer, which made them attractive to other agencies. The services also provided the project workers with more time. For example, the introduction of an elder abuse aide in Syracuse, or a homemaker in Worcester, allowed for monitoring of cases to take place without constant involvement by project staff. Without services to offer, an imbalanced exchange can develop between a project and the agencies with which it interacts. Such an imbalance can impair interagency relations.

4. *Interagency coordination is critical to the success of a project.* No single agency has all of the resources to resolve difficult cases of elder abuse. Therefore, cooperation between agencies is perhaps the most critical contributor to the success or failure of a project. All relevant community agencies should be involved from the very beginning in the design of a community elder abuse intervention, including the decision as to where it should be located. Formal coordination mechanisms should be used, such as an advisory task force and written agreements between agencies. Informal case coordination should be facilitated by team meetings and case conferences. The overwhelming weight of the evidence we have presented on the Model Projects points to the crucial importance of mutually supportive, harmonious relations among agencies concerned with elder abuse.

5. *The existence of a mandatory reporting statute without sufficient appropriations can hinder elder abuse intervention.* It appears from the evaluation of the Model Projects that the mandatory reporting statute caused serious problems for the Rhode Island project. Some critics of mandatory reporting (see Crystal 1986) have noted that states feel that they have done

their job after the law is passed, and fail to provide sufficient funds for
services to victims and abusers. In such cases, a small staff must attempt
to handle the large number of referrals that come in response to the law.
In Rhode Island, other agencies reported that they often made reports
only to conform with the law, and felt quite able to handle many of those
cases. Nevertheless, the Model Project was obligated to conduct an often
time-consuming investigation. Instead of being able to spend time on a
small group of cases that would truly benefit from their intervention, Rhode
Island staff were spread thin by investigatory duties.

   In sum, in spite of limitations in the data, the experience of the Model
Projects can provide guidance in planning elder abuse services. This experience highlights the need for a careful determination of the appropriate agency for a project, as well as attention to the services that will be
offered. As we discuss in more detail below, the findings of the Model
Projects evaluation also cast doubt on the desirability of mandatory reporting legislation for elder abuse.

FUTURE DIRECTIONS FOR RESEARCH

This project has provided a number of useful insights of value to researchers. We present the most important of these here.

   1. Investigators can confidently design studies based on direct interviews with abused elders. Victims will talk, and often at great length,
about the maltreatment. Failing to interview victims in investigations on
elder abuse can no longer be justified. While assessment data compiled
by competent professionals may accurately describe certain aspects of the
case, understanding of the family dynamics that produced mistreatment
ultimately relies on direct interviews with the parties involved.

   2. Researchers in this field should study abusers. The findings of the
present study are necessarily incomplete, in that they involved no interviews with perpetrators, whose accounts may differ greatly from those of
the victims. Since the completion of the Model Project evaluation, a study
based on interviews with perpetrators has been conducted by Anetzberger
(1987), although the small sample size calls into question the generaliz-
ability of the results. Such studies are greatly needed to more fully understand elder abuse.

   3. Future studies must move away from agency samples to general population surveys. The results of Pillemer and Finkelhor's (1988) preva-

lence survey of one metropolitan area show that agency caseloads are not necessarily representative of the types or number of cases in the population. A national incidence survey is greatly needed to learn the magnitude of the problem and to provide a more complete picture of conflict and violence. Further, a national voluntary reporting system, with standards accepted by the states for reporting of cases, is needed to provide a national profile of reported cases.

4. The importance of control group designs cannot be overemphasized. It was only through this methodology that certain characteristics of the victims were identified. For instance, the findings that physically abused elders are often less impaired than nonabused elders, and that perpetrators are more dependent than caregivers of non-abused persons, were only obtainable through a case-control study.

5. Research in this field should begin to focus to a greater degree than was done here on the consequences of abuse. What effects does being an elder abuse victim have on an individual? "Learned helplessness" has been held to result from wife abuse (Walker 1977–78, 1984). Does this hold true for abused elders? Our analyses focused on the causes of maltreatment; others should concentrate on the outcomes of abuse and neglect.

6. Investigators should pay more attention to the context of abusive acts than was done here. Does an argument precede abuse? Has one or both persons been drinking prior to the incident? Are others ever present? More specifics regarding the circumstances in which domestic violence against the elderly occur are necessary.

7. Another topic for exploration is why abusive children come to live with their parents. In this study, for example, a number of children had returned to their parents' homes after the children became divorced or separated. How frequently does this occur? In other instances, the child had severe emotional problems and could not live independently. Since fewer than one in ten elderly persons reside with their children, it may be helpful to understand how these shared living arrangements come about.

8. The findings, and particularly those regarding physical abuse, raise the question of parent-child relationships and child-rearing practices. Some of the case studies in which the adult child was dependent on the parent revealed a parent who did not "let go." What can parents do as the child is growing up to insure that the kind of pathological dependency illustrated here is avoided? The study of elder abuse can shed light beyond the specific phenomenon and can increase understanding of family relationships in a more general way.

9. Our major outcome criterion, "case resolution," needs further delineation. The simple definition of "alleviation or elimination of maltreatment" that was utilized in this project may not be adequate, especially when the victim does not wish to be separated from the perpetrator. A more valid and reliable measure for such cases may be necessary. Also of interest would be the long-term effectiveness of the approaches used by the three Model Projects. For example, did the more intensive involvement of the Worcester staff lead to a more permanent case resolution than the procedures utilized by the other two projects?

10. The concept of "neglect" requires more clarification. It assumes that family members are responsible for one another even if they are living in separate households. Willful withholding of medication, food, and other necessities by a family member can seriously threaten the life of an older person who may not be in condition to obtain them on his or her own. Such acts, in our opinion, constitute "maltreatment." But even in cases where a person has been identified as the primary caregiver, it is difficult to assign legal responsibility. When a caregiver is incapable of carrying out these tasks either because of physical, mental or cognitive impairment, the issues become even more complex. Is is helpful to label these cases, "passive neglect," as was done in this study, or is there a risk in placing the blame on individuals (e.g., the physically or mentally ill, retarded, alcoholic) whom society has failed to help?

11. Finally, the topic of elder spouse abuse needs further investigation. Until now, it has not received much attention either from those involved in the study of elder abuse or those engaged in research on spouse abuse (see Pillemer and Finkelhor 1988 for an exception). Traditionally, these two groups have worked separately, yet the experiences of both may be helpful in addressing not only the long-term abuse situations but also those that begin in later life.

FUTURE DIRECTIONS FOR PRACTICE AND POLICY

Two major issues for practioners and policymakers emerged from the Model Projects study. The first relates to what has become a favored response to elder abuse: mandatory reporting statutes. We begin our discussion with a review of this issue, and then note the implications of the present study for the debate over mandatory reporting. The second issue relates to needed service options for elder abuse victims and their families. The Model Projects evaluation provides guidance in this area as well.

Mandatory reporting

Currently, forty-three states have established statewide mandatory reporting requirements. The laws identify fifty different professionals, job titles, and groups of persons who are required to report. Most often cited are the health and helping professions, such as physicians, surgeons, nurses, social workers and law enforcement personnel, although fourteen laws require anyone to report abuse who has reasonable cause to believe that it has occurred. The agencies authorized to receive reports are most often the state welfare or social service department, and less frequently law enforcement agencies, local social service agencies, and state units on aging. Usually, the agency designated to receive reports has the responsibility for investigation.

As we noted in chapter 1, the passage of such laws has been a common response by states to elder abuse. However, elder abuse legislation is not without controversy (Faulkner 1982; Callahan 1982; Crystal 1986). Besides the fact that most laws were not accompanied by budget appropriations, other concerns of a more fundamental nature have been raised. Perhaps most important, there is no evidence as yet that mandatory reporting is effective. In fact, an early study (Alliance 1981) concluded that the increase in the number of reports filed with the authorized agencies was more likely a result of the increase in publicity about the problem of elder abuse (including the passage of the legislation) than the mandatory reporting provisions of the laws. Further, penalties for nonreporting are rarely, if ever, utilized.

Critics of mandatory elder abuse reporting believe that in using the child abuse model, proponents are adopting a set of assumptions that are not applicable to older people. Palincsar and Cobb (1982), argue that mandatory reporting laws for suspected incidents of child abuse are based on three assumptions: "(1) children are incompetent, helpless, and vulnerable; (2) children are at the mercy of their caretakers; and (3) society has a protectible interest in children" (433). The implications drawn from the analogy to child abuse are that elders are incompetent and unable to report themselves. Such inferences infantilize the elder's position in society, foster negative stereotypes of the aged, and limit older persons' ability to control their own lives (Lee 1986:731). Some elders make a competent decision to remain in an abusive situation, perhaps because they fear the alternative, but often because they have adjusted, on their own terms, to the situation, as terrible as it may appear to an outsider.

Legal questions have been raised regarding definitions, which are so broad that they may be found unconstitutional (Faulkner 1982; Crystal 1987), and the groups to be covered, which often equate age with disability and dependency. Further, by defining in an overly broad manner the class of persons who are required to report, the impact and enforceability of the laws are diminished (Lee 1986). In addition, many of the persons mandated to report are also subject to a statutory privilege, making their communication with their clients or patients confidential. The law presents these professionals with a dilemma: either to violate the law, or break the trust of a client and possibly jeopardize a therapeutic relationship. Paradoxically, the law may keep the victims from seeking help, for fear of being reported.

Thus, a major controversy exists over mandatory reporting. What insights have we gained from the Model Projects on this issue? In fact, the findings presented in earlier chapters appear to cast doubt on the effectiveness of this option. The project that operated under mandatory reporting—Rhode Island—experienced problems that can be attributed to the statute.

In particular, the project was inundated with referrals, all of which had to be investigated. The law encouraged persons in other agencies to report all potential cases, regardless of how remote the possibility of abuse or neglect. The number of staff necessary to carry out such a large number of investigations was greater than Rhode Island (or most other states), was able to provide. Staff were unable to focus on the most serious cases, which led to worker frustration, as well as to dissatisfaction on the part of other agencies.

Further, because of the need for speedy response to reports, staff in Rhode Island were not able to devote as much time to individual cases as were the other projects. They also did not have the flexibility in dealing with cases that was evident in the other projects. Finally, the referral data show that Rhode Island did not receive a greater number of reports from many categories of mandatory reporters than did the other projects (see table 6.1).

Clearly, these findings are by no means grounds upon which to definitively reject mandatory reporting. However, the present study should be added to the growing number of voices that urge caution regarding this response to elder abuse. Such statutes *must* be carefully evaluated to determine their effectiveness. At the very least, the Model Projects evaluation provides evidence that mandatory reporting for elder abuse is not a solution in itself, but must be accompanied by a substantial commitment of resources to the designated reporting agency.

Implications for service delivery

The finding that abusers are less likely to be stressed caregivers than they are to be troubled and impaired individuals has important implications for service planning. Previous attempts to identify older persons at high risk of abuse have been colored by the assumption that the dependency of the victim causes maltreatment. The results reported here point to a more important risk category: situations in which relatives live as dependents with the older person. Elder abuse workers and other professionals should pay special attention to such cases.

Based on the hypothesis that the dependency of victims leads to abuse, supportive services have been offered to caregivers. In many cases of elder abuse, an attempt is made to introduce home care services, such as housekeeping and meal preparation, to relieve the "burden" of caregiving. Although such services may play a role in preventing or ameliorating abuse situations, the present study shows a need for other services as well.

Social exchange theory offers an approach to intervention. Either the rewards of reducing dependency on the elder can be increased or the costs of abusing the victim can be heightened. To achieve the former goal, unhealthy dependence of a relative on an older person could be reduced through psychotherapy, employment counseling, and financial support for the abuser while he or she establishes an independent household. In some cases, the change in living situation may be a nursing home placement for a dependent, abusive spouse.

The costs of abusing an elderly person can be raised in a variety of ways. One option is to increase social support for the elderly. For example, the battered women's movement, as noted earlier, has made much use of self-help groups. One important component of such groups has been consciousness-raising. Battered women and their advocates have gone to great lengths to convey to group members that they have a right to be free from violence, and that its use cannot be justified. These women then convey this message to their spouses. With support, they become able to say: "I will not take this anymore."

Such an approach has been used by the Elder Abuse Project sponsored by the Victims Services Agency of New York City. This program, known as "A Safe Place" offers support groups to older victims of abuse and neglect. Membership in a support group is limited to competent elderly persons, 60 years of age and over, who have been abused by a relative. Although the project is open to men as well as women, group members have usually been female. The program creates a hospitable, nonjudgmental environment with clinical and peer support in which victims can share their own problems and explore options to improve their situation.

There are two leaders at the weekly group meetings: a staff person who focuses primarily on the instructive aspects of the group process and a senior volunteer, who facilitates the expressive aspects. The senior volunteer, as a peer, represents a model of an older person living a life without violence. During the sessions, members have the opportunity to talk with other abuse victims in the group and to establish relationships of mutual support. They also generate ideas to help each other solve problems. From this sharing, a bond between individuals who had previously felt isolated grows. Individual needs are addressed and people are able to change or improve the abuse situation in some way.

Still another possibility for increasing the costs of abusive behavior is the use of "safe houses" or emergency shelters by elderly victims. Battered women's advocates have relied heavily on such locations to protect abused victims. This model presumes that after escaping from the abuse, the victim can either begin to live independently, or can return to the abuser, who becomes aware that she will no longer tolerate abuse. Often cited as a much-needed resource for helping elderly victims, emergency shelters of various types and forms are being developed in communities both here and abroad.

One of the first shelters designed specifically for the elderly has been reported by the shelter movement in Finland (Heinanen 1986). Working with local elder service providers, three domestic violence shelters undertook a cooperative project that made use of beds in a nursing home facility. Other examples include the adult foster home project established by the Central Vermont Council on Aging in Barre, Vermont and the group home organized by three county departments of social services in South Carolina.

In instances where the victim refuses to leave the household, attempts can be made to increase the presence of outsiders. Strengthening the informal support network can increase the costs of abusive behavior to the perpetrator, for interested outsiders are able to negatively sanction the behavior. Informal support networks can be built up through volunteers, by creating linkages in neighborhoods, and through case management programs (Biegel et al. 1984).

A final alternative is legal action. Obviously, when elder abuse was conceived as occurring because of caregiver strain, involving the police rarely seemed necessary. In the new conceptualization put forth here, physical elder abuse is seen as having parallels with spouse abuse: relatively independent people sharing a residence with the physically stronger one victimizing the weaker. In fact, legal action may be especially appropriate in elder abuse cases that involve financial exploitation. In the Model Project study, legal measures were used in 36 percent of these cases.

Sherman and Berk (1984) have provided important (although somewhat controversial) evidence that police intervention may reduce the incidence of domestic violence. In one experiment, they found that arrest was the most effective method to prevent further episodes of wife abuse. If the traditional police reluctance to get involved in domestic violence can be overcome, such law enforcement activity in elder abuse may also be effective. The cost of being arrested for many would greatly outweigh the rewards obtained from abusive behavior. There are other ways in which the police can become involved, as well. They are often the first people on the scene in response to a complaint of elder abuse and therefore may be in a unique position to intervene if necessary.

An example is provided by the Charleston, South Carolina, police department. It sponsors a telephone line designated specifically to assist in the protection of older citizens, and has widely circulated the hotline number through mailings and the mass media. Although the line functions mainly as a referral service using volunteer operators, the fact that it is located in the police department is viewed as an advantage. In particular, response time to emergencies can be minimized by quickly dispatching a police cruiser to the scene of the complaint and then notifying the department of social services.

Police departments are only one of many types of community agencies that are becoming concerned with the problem of elder abuse and neglect. As this evaluation has shown, it is vitally important to be able to mobilize many different agencies on behalf of the abused or neglected client. The methods just described can help create necessary interagency linkages. Many more efforts along these lines are underway throughout the country. In attempting to respond to the needs of abused and neglected elderly, communities have created task forces of service providers and other interested individuals. These groups attempt to raise the consciousness of professionals and lay people regarding the needs of abused and neglected elders.

Among the best organized of these task forces is the San Francisco Consortium for Elder Abuse Prevention, which began in 1981. The task force has established goals and objectives for a service delivery program that includes outreach, training, coordination, service development, and advocacy. It also has defined the roles and responsibilities of the various program components, including a formal network of member agencies, a steering committee, a multidisciplinary team and a coordinating agency.

Forty-five member agencies are represented in the Consortium. Upon joining, an agency signs "linkage" agreements in which they agree to: 1) train their staff in elder abuse awareness; 2) accept client referrals; 3) share information; and 4) abide by a set of guidelines for fund-raising to encourage cooperation rather than competition among member agencies.

When a service provider contacts Mt. Zion Hospital and Medical Center—the consortium's coordinating agency—on behalf of a client, the program coordinator may suggest particular interventions or refer the service provider to another consortium member agency. If a case requires collaborative assessment, the provider will be directed to the multidisciplinary team for case consultation. Each case is presented to the team by the client's service provider or program coordinator, who also does the case follow-up and reports to the team regarding the resolution of the case. The consortium believes that the team is important because it reduces the potential for case plans to become skewed in the direction of a single agency worker's professional expertise and assures that situations are evaluated from the perspective of all the disciplines represented.

The above examples, of which many more could be cited, represent exciting steps in the effort to prevent and treat elder abuse and neglect. In fact, based on the Model Projects evaluation, it is our belief that such local, community-based projects are the key to successful intervention. Rather than mandatory reporting legislation and protective services, the real solution to elder abuse and neglect appears to us to lie in the development of a comprehensive service system to meet the needs of victims and their families.

SOME FINAL THOUGHTS

At the outset of this book we raised the question of the limits of family responsibility for the elderly. Many individuals caring for severly impaired relatives do so willingly and competently. However, the data on the abuse victims provide a picture of families in trouble. Some involved caregivers who were under tremendous stress; in other cases, relatives had a variety of personal difficulties that eventually resulted in maltreatment.

In light of these findings, federal and state attempts to shift even more responsibility to relatives should be carefully evaluated. Such plans range from providing a direct payment to persons caring for aged relatives in their home, to actually making children liable for the costs of their parents' nursing home care. Based on the data presented in this book, such a shifting of responsibility should be done only with great caution. Put simply, some family members do not have the ability to care for frail, impaired older persons. Policies that place the elderly in the hands of such individuals must be pursued with care. Certainly, concomitant with any such steps must be the provision of protective services. As part of that effort, new and better ways of screening and identifying potentially abusive households must be developed.

Also to be resisted is the tendency to fall back on the child abuse model as a framework for intervention and prevention. Most of the findings from the various analyses do not correspond to those identified with child abuse. The sociocultural variables were not primary risk factors; evidence to support the "cycle of violence" theory was not conclusive. More important, the significant amount of abuse perpetrated by spouses, and of financial exploitation by relatives and nonrelatives, represent entirely different family and interpersonal dynamics than those associated with child abuse. And yet, elder abuse policy (to the degree that it exists) has been modeled after child abuse. Reconceptualization of the problem as domestic violence, with voluntary reporting and the involvement of service providers who function as victim advocates, reflect more accurately the nature of the problem as it has been defined in this study.

Finally, in chapter 1 we responded to critics who question whether elder abuse is a meaningful concept around which to organize practice and policy. They have suggested that the aged would be better served by focusing attention on improving income maintenance, medical care, and social service programs for the benefit of all vulnerable elders. These are, to be sure, worthy goals. In light of the findings from the Model Projects evaluation, however, we hold that our society must address elder abuse and neglect as important social problems.

The interviews with victims and the exposure to hundreds of cases have convinced us that these families constitute a special category and cannot be helped through ordinary means. Further, to insist that we wait until policymakers are ready to expand social welfare and health programs in this country to eliminate the root causes of elder maltreatment is unrealistic. What we can most optimistically hope for is that the incremental approach to policy formulation will at least help the most seriously abused aged persons, and that steps toward prevention will be taken. The lessons learned in responding to the needs of abused and neglected elders may in turn serve as guideposts for advancing the quality of life for all older adults and their families.

Bibliography

Adams, Bert N. 1968. *Kinship in an Urban Setting*. Chicago: Markham.

Administration on Aging. 1980. *Guidelines for Preparation of Grant Applications*. Title IV-C Model Projects. Washington, D.C.: GPO.

Alliance Elder Abuse Project. 1981. "An Analysis of State's Mandatory Reporting Laws on Elder Abuse." Syracuse, N.Y.: Alliance/Catholic Charities. Manuscript.

American Public Welfare Association and the National Association of State Units on Aging Elder Abuse Project. 1986. *A Comprehensive Analysis of State Policy and Practice Related to Elder Abuse*. Washington, D.C.: American Public Welfare Association and National Association of State Units on Aging.

Andrews F. M. and S. B. Withey. 1979. *Social Indicators of Well-Being: Americans' Perceptions of Life Quality*. New York: Plenum.

Anetzberger, Georgia. 1987. *The Etiology of Elder Abuse by Adult Offspring*. Springfield, Ill.: Charles C Thomas.

Atchley, R. C. 1987. *The Social Forces in Later Life: An Introduction to Social Gerontology*. Belmont, Calif.: Wadsworth.

Baruch G. and R. C. Barnett. 1983. "Adult Daughters' Relationships with Their Mothers." *Journal of Marriage and the Family* 45:601–606.

Bergman, James A., ed. 1981. "Abuse of Older Persons: Report of the First National Conference on Abuse of Older Persons." Boston: Legal Research and Services for the Elderly.

Biegel, D. E., B. K. Shore, and E. Gordon. 1984. *Building Support Networks for the Elderly: Theory and Applications*. Beverly Hills, Calif.: Sage.

Block, Marilyn R. and Jan D. Sinnott. 1979. *The Battered Elder Syndrome: An Exploratory Study*. College Park, Md.: University of Maryland, Center on Aging.

Breckman, Risa and Ronald Adelman. 1988. *Strategies for Helping Victims of Elder Mistreatment*. Beverly Hills, Calif.: Sage.

Bristowe, Elizabeth. 1987. "Family Mediated Abuse of Non-Institutionalized Frail Elderly Men and Women Living in British Columbia." Paper presented at the Third National Conference for Family Violence Researchers, July, Durham, N.H.

Brody, Elaine M. 1985. "The Informal Support System and Health of the Future Aged." In C. M. Gaitz ed., *Aging 2000: Our Health Care Destiny*. Vol. 2: *Psychological and Policy Issues*. New York: Springer.

Brubaker, Timothy H. 1985. *Later Life Families*. Beverly Hills, Calif.: Sage.

Butler, Robert. 1975. *Why Survive? Being Old in America*. New York: Harper and Row.

Caffey, J. 1946. "Multiple Fractures in the Long Bones of Children Suffering from Chronic Subdural Hematoma." *American Journal of Roentgenology* 56:53–58.

Callahan, James J. 1981. "Elder Abuse Programming: Will It Help the Elderly?" Paper presented at the National Conference on the Abuse of Older Persons. Boston.

Callahan, James J. 1982. "Elder Abuse Programming: Will It Help the Elderly?" *Urban and Social Change Review* 15:15–19.

Callahan, James J. 1986. "Guest Editor's Perspective." *Pride Institute Journal of Long-Term Home Health Care* 5:2–3.

Cantor, Marjorie H. 1983. "Strain Among Caregivers: A Study of Experience in the United States." *Gerontologist* 23:597–604.

Chodorow, Nancy. 1978. *The Reproduction of Mothering*. Berkeley: University of California Press.

Cicirelli, Victor G. 1981. *Helping Elderly Parents: The Role of Adult Children*. Boston: Auburn House.

Cicirelli, Victor G. 1983a. "Adult Children and Their Parents." In T. H. Brubaker, ed., *Family Relationships in Later Life*. Beverly Hills, Calif.: Sage.

Cicirelli, Victor G. 1983b. "Adult Children's Attachment and Helping Behavior to Elderly Parents: A Path Model." *Journal of Marriage and the Family* 45:815–825.

Cicirelli, Victor G. 1986. "The Helping Relationship and Family Neglect in Later Life." In K. A. Pillemer and R. S. Wolf, eds., *Elder Abuse: Conflict in the Family*, pp. 49–66. Dover, Mass.: Auburn House.

Cobb, S. 1976. "Social Support as a Moderator of Life Stress." *Psychosomatic Medicine* 38:300–312.

Cohler, B. J. 1983. "Autonomy and Interdependence in the Family of Adulthood: A Psychological Perspective." *Gerontologist* 23:33–39.

Coleman, D. and M. A. Straus. 1981. "Alcohol Abuse and Family Violence." Durham, N.H.: University of New Hampshire, Family Violence Research Program.

Cravedi, Kathleen Gardner. 1986. "Elder abuse: The Evolution of Federal and State Policy Reform." *Pride Institute Journal of Long Term Home Health Care* 5:4–9.

Crouse, Joyce S., Deborah C. Kobb, Britta B. Harris, Frank J. Kopecky, and John Poertner. 1981. *Abuse and Neglect of the Elderly in Illinois*. Springfield: Illinois Department on Aging.

Crystal, S. 1986. "Social policy and elder abuse." In K. A. Pillemer and R. S. Wolf, eds., *Elder Abuse: Conflict in the Family*. Dover, Mass.: Auburn House.

Davidson, Janice L. 1979. "Elder Abuse." In M. R. Block and J. D. Sinnott, eds., *The Battered Elder Syndrome: An Exploratory Study*. Center on Aging, University of Maryland.

Davidson B., J. Balswick, and C. Halverson. 1983. "Affective Self-Disclosure and Marital Adjustment: A Test of Equity Theory." *Journal of Marriage and the Family* 45:93–102.

Dobash, R. Emerson and Russell P. Dobash. 1979. *Violence Against Wives: A Case Against the Patriarchy*. New York: Free Press.

Douglas, Richard L., Tom Hickey, and Catherine Noel. 1980. A *Study of Maltreatment of the Elderly and Other Vulnerable Adults*. Ann Arbor: University of Michigan, Institute of Gerontology.

Dowd, J. J. 1975. "Aging and Exchange: A Preface to Theory." *Journal of Gerontology* 30:584–594.

Dworkin, Andrea. 1974. *Woman Hating*. New York: Dutton.

Duke University Center for the Study of Aging and Human Development. 1979. *Multidimensional Functional Assessment: The OARS Methodology*. Durham, N.C.: Duke University.

Faulk, M. 1974. "Men Who Assault Their Wives." *Medicine, Science, and the Law* 14:80–183.

Faulkner, Lawrence R. 1982. "Mandating the Reporting of Suspected Cases of Elder Abuse: An Inappropriate, Ineffective, and Ageist Response to the Abuse of Older Adults." *Family Law Quarterly* 16:69–91.

Finkelhor, David. 1983. "Common Features of Family Abuse." In D. Finkelhor, R. J. Gelles, G. Hotaling, and M. Straus, eds., *The Dark Side of Families: Current Family Violence Research*, pp. 17–26. Beverly Hills, Calif.: Sage.

Finkelhor, David and Karl Pillemer, 1984. "Elder Abuse: Its Relationship to Other Forms of Domestic Violence." Paper presented at the Second National Conference on Family Violence Research, July, Durham, N.H.

Finkelhor, David and Karl Pillemer. 1987. "Correlates of Elder Abuse: A Case Control Study." Paper presented at the Third National Conference for Family Violence Researchers. July, Durham, N.H.

Finkelhor, David and Kersti Yllo. 1983. "Rape in Marriage: A Sociological View." In D. Finkelhor, R. S. Gelles, G. T. Hotaling, and M. A. Straus, eds., *The Dark Side of Families*, pp. 119–130. Beverly Hills, CA: Sage.

Foner, Nancy. 1985. "Caring for the Elderly: A Cross-Cultural View." In B. B. Hess and E. W. Markson, eds., *Growing Old in America*, pp. 71–85. New Brunswick: Transaction.

Gelles, Richard J. 1972. *The Violent Home*. Beverly Hills, Calif.: Sage.

Gelles, Richard J. 1974. "Child Abuse as Psychopathology: A Sociological Critique and Reformulation." In S. Steinmetz and M. A. Straus, eds., *Violence in the Family*, pp. 190–204. New York: Dodd, Mead.

Gelles, Richard J. and Murray A. Straus. 1979a. "Determinants of Violence in the Family: Toward a Theoretical Integration." In W. R. Burr, R. Hill, F. I. Nye, and I. L. Reiss, eds., *Contemporary Theories About the Family*. New York: Free Press.

George, Linda K. 1986. "Caregiver Burden: Conflict Between Norms of Reciprocity and Solidarity. In K. A. Pillemer and R. S. Wolf, eds., *Elder Abuse: Families in Conflict*. Dover, Mass. Auburn House.

Gil, David G. 1971. *Violence Against Children: Physical Child Abuse in the United States*. Cambridge: Harvard University Press.

Gioglio, G. R. and P. Blakemore. 1983. "Elder Abuse in New Jersey: The Knowledge and Experience of Abuse Among Older New Jerseyans." Trenton: New Jersey Department of Human Services.

Glascock, Anthony and Susan Feinman. 1981. "Social Asset or Social Burden: An Analysis of the Treatment of the Aged in Non-Industrial Societies." In Christine L. Fry, ed., *Dimensions: Aging, Culture and Health*. New York: Praeger.

Glenn, N. and C. Weaver. 1981. "A Multivariate, Multisurvey Study of Marital Happiness." *Journal of Marriage and the Family* 40:269–282.

Guilford, Rosalie. 1986. "Marriage in Later Life." *Generations* (Summer), pp. 16–20.

Heinanen, Aira. 1986. *Domestic Violence and the Elderly*. Helsinki, Finland: Ensi Kotien Liitto.

Hendricks, J. and C. D. Hendricks. 1981. *Aging in Mass Society: Myths and Realities*. Cambridge: Winthrop.

Hennesey, S. 1979. "Child Abuse." In M. R. Block and J. D. Sinnott, eds., *The Battered Elder Syndrome: An Exploratory Study*. College Park, Md: University of Maryland, Center on Aging.

Hickey, Tom. 1980. *Health and Aging*. Monterey, Calif.: Brooks/Cole.

Holmes, T. H. and R. H. Rahe. 1967. "The Social Readjustment Rating Scale." *Journal of Psychosomatic Research* 11:213–218.

Hotaling G. and D. Sugarman. 1986. "An Analysis of Risk Markers in Husband to Wife Violence: The Current State of Knowledge." *Violence and Victims* 1:101–124.

Hudson, Margaret and Tanya Johnson. 1987. "Elder Neglect and Abuse: A Review of the Literature." In Carl Eisdorfer, ed., *Annual Review of Gerontology*. New York: Springer.

Hudson, Robert B. and Robert Binstock. 1976. "Political Systems and Aging." R. H. Binstock and E. Shanas, eds., *Handbook of Aging and the Social Sciences*. New York: Van Nostrand Reinhold.

Hwalek, Melanie A., Mary C. Sengstock, and R. Lawrence. 1984. "Assessing the Probability of Abuse of the Elderly." Paper presented at the Annual Meeting of the Gerontological Society of America, November, Dallas, Texas.

IDA (Illinois Department on Aging). 1987. Elder Abuse Demonstration Project. Third Interim Report to the Illinois General Assembly on Public Acts 83-1259 and 83-1432. Springfield, Ill.

Johnson, Colleen L. 1985. "The Impact of Illness on Late-life Marriages." *Journal of Marriage and the Family* 47:165–172.

Johnson, E. S. and B. J. Bursk. 1977. "Relationships Between the Elderly and Their Adult Children." *Gerontologist* 17:90–96.

Johnson, Tanya. 1986. "Critical Issues in the Definition of Elder Mistreatment." In *Elder Abuse: Conflict in the Family*, pp. 167–195. Dover, Mass.: Auburn House.

Johnson, Tanya, James G. O'Brien, and Margaret F. Hudson. 1985. *Elder Neglect and Abuse: An Annotated Bibliography*. Westport, Conn.: Greenwood Press.

Justice, Blair and Rita Justice. 1976. *The Abusing Family*. New York: Human Sciences Press.

Kalmuss, Debra S. and Murray A. Straus. 1983. "Feminist, Political, and Economic Determinants of Wife Abuse Services in American States." In Finkelhor et al., eds., *The Dark Side of Families: Current Family Violence Research*. Beverly Hills, Calif.: Sage.

Kantor G. and M. Straus. 1986. "Substance Abuse as a Precipitant of Family Violence Victimization." Paper presented at the American Society of Criminology Meeting. Atlanta.

Kempe, Henry, Frederic N. Silverman, Brandt T. Steele, William Droegemueller, and Henry K. Silver. 1962. "The Battered Child Syndrome." *Journal of the American Medical Association* 181:17–24.

Korbin, Jill, Kevin J. Eckert, Georgia Anetzberger, Elizabeth Whitmore, Lisa Mitchell, and Edith Vargo. 1987. "Elder Abuse and Child Abuse: Commonalities and Differences." Paper presented at the Third National Conference for Family Violence Researchers. July, Durham, N.H.

Kruse, Andreas. 1986. "Caring For a Chronically Ill Family Member—Family Conflict and Possibilities of Intervention." Paper presented at the Workshop on Stress, Conflict, and Abuse in the Aging Family, 30th Anniversary of the Israel Gerontological Society, August, Jerusalem, Israel.

Lasch, Christopher. 1977. *Haven in a Heartless World: The Family Besieged.* New York: Basic Books.

Laslett, Peter. 1965. *The World We Have Lost.* London: Methuen.

Lau, Elizabeth and Jordan Kosberg. 1979. "Abuse of the Elderly by Informal Care Providers." *Aging* 10–15.

Lee, Dyana. 1985–1986. "Mandatory Reporting of Elder Abuse: A Cheap But Ineffective Solution to the Problem." *Fordham Urban Law Journal* 14:725–771.

Lee, G. 1978. "Marriage and Morale in Later Life." *Journal of Marriage and the Family* 40:131–139.

Levin, J. and W. C. Levin. 1980. *Ageism: Prejudice and Discrimination Against the Elderly.* Belmont, Calif.: Wadsworth.

Lion, J. R. 1977. "Clinical Aspects of Wifebattering." In M. Roy, ed., *Battered Women*, pp. 126–136. New York: Van Nostrand Reinhold.

Luetz, Walter N., Jay N. Greenberg, Ruby Abrahams, Jeffrey Prottas, Larry M. Diamond, and Leonard Gruenberg. 1985. *Changing Health Care for an Aging Society.* Lexington, Mass.: Lexington Books.

Morris, John N., Sylvia Sherwood, and Vincent Mor, 1984. "An Assessment Tool for Use in Identifying Functionally Vulnerable Persons in the Community." *Gerontologist* 24:373–79.

Morris, L. L. and C. T. Fitzgibbon. 1978. *How to Measure Program Implementation.* Beverly Hills, Calif.: Sage.

Myers, Laura. 1980. "Battered Wives, Dead Husbands." In A. Skolnick and J. Skolnick, eds., *Family in Transition Third Edition*, pp. 333–340. Boston: Little, Brown.

Nelson, Barbara J. 1984. *Making an Issue of Child Abuse.* Chicago: University of Chicago Press.

Newberger, Eli H. and Richard Bourne. 1978. "The Medicalization and Legalization of Child Abuse." *American Journal of Orthopsychiatry* 48:593–607.

Newell, D. S. 1961. "Social Structural Evidence for Disengagement." In E. Cumming and W. F. Henry, eds., *Growing Old.* New York: Basic Books.

Nydegger, Corinne N. 1983. "Family Ties of the Aged in Cross-Cultural Perspective." In B. B. Hess and Elizabeth W. Markson, eds., *Growing Old in America*, pp. 387–400. New Brunswick, N.J.: Transaction.

Nye, I. F. 1979. "Choice, Exchange, and the Family." In W. R. Burr, R. Hill, F. I. Nye, and I. L. Reiss, eds., *Contemporary Theories About the Family*, pp. 1–41. New York: Free Press.

O'Malley, Helen, Howard Segars, Ruben Perez, Victoria Mitchell, and George M. Knuepfel. 1979. *Elder Abuse in Massachusetts: A Survey of Professionals and Paraprofessionals.* Boston: Legal Research and Services for the Elderly.

O'Malley, Terrance, Helen C. O'Malley, Daniel E. Everitt, and Deborah Sarson. 1986. "Categories of Family Mediated Abuse and Neglect of Elderly Persons. *Journal of the American Geriatrics Society* 32:362–369.

Palinscar, John and Deborah Crouse Cobb. 1982. "The Physician's Role in Detecting and Reporting Elder Abuse." *Journal of Legal Medicine* 3:413–42.

Pedrick-Cornell, C. and R. J. Gelles. 1982. "Elder Abuse: The Status of Current Knowledge." *Family Relations* 31:457–65.

Phillips, Linda R. 1983. "Abuse and Neglect of the Frail Elderly at Home: An Exploration of Theoretical Relationships." *Journal of Advanced Nursing* 8:379–92.

Pillemer, Karl. 1985a. "Domestic Violence Against the Elderly: A Case-Control Study." Ph.D. dissertation, Brandeis University, Waltham, Mass.

Pillemer, Karl. 1985b. "The Dangers of Dependency: New Findings on Domestic Violence Against the Elderly." Social Problems 33:146–158.

Pillemer, Karl. 1986. "Risk Factors in Elder Abuse: Results From a Case-Control Study." In K. A. Pillemer and R. S. Wolf, eds., Elder Abuse: Conflict in the Family, pp. 239–263. Dover, Mass.: Auburn House.

Pillemer, Karl. 1987. "Merging Qualitative and Quantitative Data in the Study of Elder Abuse." In S. Reinharz and G. Rowles, eds., Qualitative Gerontology. New York: Springer.

Pillemer, Karl and David Finkelhor. 1988. "Prevalence of Elder Abuse: A Random Sample Survey." Gerontologist 28:51–57.

Pillemer Karl and J. Jill Suitor. 1988. "Elder Abuse." In V. Van Hasselt et al., eds., Handbook of Family Violence. New York: Plenum.

Quinn, Mary Joy and Susan Tomita. 1986. Elder Abuse and Neglect: Causes, Diagnosis, and Intervention Strategies. New York: Springer.

Radbill, Samuel X. 1975. "A History of Child Abuse and Infanticide." In S. Steinmetz and M. Straus, eds., Violence in the Family. New York: Dodd, Mead.

Reichel, W. 1978. "Multiple Problems in the Elderly." In W. Reichel, ed., The Geriatric Patient. Tucson: HP Books.

Reinharz, Shulamit. 1986. "Loving and Hating One's Elders: Twin Themes in Legend and Literature." In K. A. Pillemer and R. S. Wolf, eds., Elder Abuse: Conflict in the Family, pp. 25–48. Dover, Mass.: Auburn House.

Salend, E., R. A. Kane, M. Satz, and Jon Pynoos. 1984. "Elder Abuse Reporting: Limitations of Statutes." Gerontologist 24:61–69.

Sengstock, Mary C. and Jersey Liang. 1982. Identifying and Characterizing Elder Abuse. Detroit: Wayne State University Institute of Gerontology.

Shainess, N. 1975. "Psychological Aspects of Wife-Battering." Birmingham Post.

Shanas, Ethel. 1979. "The Family as a Support System in Old Age." Gerontologist, 19:3–9.

Sherman, Lawrence W. and Richard A. Berk. 1984. "The Minneapolis Domestic Violence Experiment." Police Foundation Reports, (April), vol. 1.

Skolnick, Arlene S. 1987. The Intimate Environment, 4th ed. Boston: Little, Brown.

Spector, M. and J. I. Kitsuse. 1977. Constructing Social Problems. Reading, Mass.: Cummings.

Stark, Evan, Ann Flitcraft, D. Zuckerman, A. Gray, J. Robinson, and W. Frazier. 1981. Wife Abuse in the Medical Setting: An Introduction to Health Personnel. Washington, D.C.: National Clearinghouse on Domestic Violence.

Stearns, Peter J. 1986. "Old Age Family Conflict: The Perspective of The Past." In K. A. Pillemer and R. S. Wolf, eds., Elder Abuse: Conflict in the Family, pp. 3–24. Dover, Mass.: Auburn House.

Steinmetz, Suzanne K. 1983. "Dependency, Stress, and Violence Between Middle-Aged Caregivers and Their Elderly Parents." In J. I. Kosberg, ed., Abuse and Maltreatment of the Elderly. Littleton, Mass.: John Wright PGS.

Steinmetz, Suzanne K. and Deborah J. Amsden. 1983. "Dependency, Family Stress, and Abuse." In T. H. Brubaker, ed., Family Relationships in Later Life, pp. 173–192. Beverly Hills, Calif.: Sage.

Straus, Murray A. 1979. "Family Patterns and Child Abuse in a Nationally Representative American Sample." In Child Abuse and Neglect, pp. 213–225.

Straus, Murray A. 1979b. "Sociological Perspective on the Causes of Family Vio-
   lence." Paper presented at the American Association for the Advancement of Sci-
   ence Annual Meeting, Houston.
Straus, Murray A. and Richard A. Gelles. 1986. "Societal Change and Change in
   Family Violence from 1975 to 1985 as Revealed by Two National Surveys." *Journal
   of Marriage and the Family* 48:465–479.
Straus, Murray, Richard J. Gelles, and Suzanne Steinmetz. 1980. *Behind Closed Doors:
   Violence in the American Family*. New York: Doubleday.
Thorne, Barrie, and Marilyn Yalom. 1982. *Rethinking the Family*. New York: Long-
   man.
Troll, Lillian, S. Miller, and Robert Atchley. 1979. *Families in Later Life*. Belmont,
   Calif.: Wadsworth.
U.S. Department of Health and Human Services. 1985. *Surgeon General's Workshop
   on Violence and Public Health Report*. Leesburg, Va.
U.S. House of Representatives: SCA (Select Committee on Aging). 1979. *Elder Abuse:
   The Hidden Problem*. Washington, D.C.: GPO.
U.S. House of Representatives: SCA. 1981. *Elder Abuse: An Examination of a Hidden
   Problem*. Washington, DC: GPO.
U.S. House of Representatives: SCA, Subcommittee on Health and Long-Term Care.
   1985. *Elder Abuse: A National Disgrace*. Washington, D.C.: GPO.
Van de Ven, Andrew H. and Diane L. Ferry. 1980. *Measuring and Assessing Organi-
   zations*. New York: Wiley.
Walker, Lenore. 1977–1978. "Battered Women and Learned Helplessness." *Victim-
   ology* 2:525–534.
Walker, Lenore. 1984. *The Battered Women Syndrome*. New York: Springer.
Wan, T. T. H. 1982. *Stressful Life Events, Social Support Networks, and Gerontological
   Health*. Lexington, Mass.: Lexington Books.
Ward, R. A. 1984. *The Aging Experience*. New York: Harper and Row.
Wolf R., Michael A. Godkin, and Karl Pillemer. 1984. *Elder Abuse and Neglect: Re-
   port from Three Model Projects*. Worcester, Mass.: University of Massachusetts Med-
   ical Center.
Wolf, Rosalie, Michael A. Godkin, and Karl Pillemer. 1984. *Elder Abuse and Neglect:
   Report from Three Model Projects*. Worcester, Mass.: University of Massachusetts
   Medical Center.
Yogev, Sara and Jeanne Brett. 1985. "Perceptions of the Division of Housework and
   Child Care and Marital Satisfaction." *Journal of Marriage and the Family* 47:609–
   618.
Young, L. 1974. "Parents Who Hate." In S. Steinmetz, and M. A. Straus, eds., *Vi-
   olence in the Family*, pp. 187–189. New York: Dodd, Mead.
Zarit, Steven H., Pamela A. Todd, and Judy M. Zarit. 1986. "Subjective Burden of
   Husbands and Wives as Caregivers: A Longitudinal Study." *Gerontologist* 26:260–
   266.

Name Index

Subject Index